Marketing Levies and Bond Issues for Public Schools

by

Gordon L. Wise
Professor of Marketing
Wright State University

Glenn T. Graham
Professor of Education
Wright State University

Duane L. Bachman
Superintendent of Schools
Piqua, Ohio, City Schools

University Monograph Number 7
Wright State University
Dayton, Ohio

LC 86-051163
ISBN 0-932429-02-5

Printed in the United States of America

Acknowledgements

The authors would like to recognize individuals who were major contributors to this effort. The body of knowledge contained here is a tribute to their hard work, inspiration, and dedication to the task at hand and, in three significant cases, to the authors.

The select group includes Beverly Pratt, Jerry Easley, Bill McNeil, and Cliff Alexander, who made the Piqua case study the success it was; Jo Ann Self and Barbara Fultz, whose long hours of typing and revising were so vital; and our wives, Susie Wise, Bettie Graham, and Mary Jane Bachman, whose encouragement and sometimes subtle pressures kept us heading toward conclusion of the manuscript. Hundreds of others could be cited among those who toiled "in the trenches" to make our plans and direction come alive.

We thank you all.

Gordon L. Wise
Glenn T. Graham
Duane L. Bachman

Contents

Abstract

Public (voter) approval is increasingly difficult to obtain for financing the operation of public schools. The proportion of school financing issues turned down at the polls has increased dramatically during the past two decades. Traditional approaches and campaigns are not working as they once did.

This study presents a marketing-based approach to this serious community problem. Drawing on rich experience, the authors developed a blueprint for the application of marketing tools, strategies, and tactics to public school levy and bond issue campaigns.

The blueprint contains an elaborate presentation applying fundamental market research to identifying key issues and high-potential strategies. It provides an explanation of marketing plan development and the strategies and tactics flowing from that plan, and it carefully addresses product development application, pricing and promotion strategies, and organizational structure development. Numerous useful examples are carefully described in the text and reproduced in the Appendices.

Although this is not a specific case study, it draws heavily on the experiences of the authors in assisting with successful campaign development for both bond issue and operating levy support.

The unique marketing approach presented here contrasts greatly with more traditional approaches often overused in school financing campaigns. It presents fresh ideas proven useful in dealing with a steadily worsening problem that has defied traditional solutions.

Chapter I

Introduction

Introduction and Overview

It is stimulating and exciting to find new ways to deal with old problems. This is particularly true if those new ways are more effective and more likely to produce results than the old or traditional approach(es) to those problems.

After decades of primary use in behalf of products and services, the rather modern art of marketing is now employed in many and diverse areas. The tools, knowledge, and skills of the marketing professional are increasingly useful in addressing critical problems of many community organizations. Churches, museums, performing arts centers, social service agencies—and school systems—are learning to apply the tried and tested marketing principles to their markets.

For some entities, help comes not a bit too soon. With a roller-coaster economy and taxpayer resistance (and even taxpayer revolts) to higher taxes, gaining acceptance of higher taxes to operate or build school facilities has gotten no easier. This holds true whether school funding increases are voted directly by residents or are approved indirectly by an elected or appointed official.

Even for the school district that seldom, if ever, asks for added financial support, the need for a modern ''product'' marketing effort is important.

With a significant background in the application of marketing tools, the authors address the ways in which the marketing art form can be recruited, controlled, financed, planned, and its success and impact evaluated.

Much of the case-type material is drawn from a single community—Piqua, Ohio, a midsized town with a population of twenty-five thousand residing in its school district. The concepts, strategies, tactics, and tools identified and used here are shown to have the broadest possible application both to districts that are forced to go to voters for added funds and to those whose funding increases are approved by boards or private individuals.

In addition, the relevance of the tools described and used in this study is equally high where there is need for identifying those elements of promotion, planning, and public relations that any functioning school system must confront.

In order to make such an application, it is necessary to examine the background of the changes that have taken place in recent years within the discipline of marketing. The scope of marketing has widened as its tools have been fine-tuned to deal with such matters as school public relations, image development/enhancement/improvement, passage of bond issues (to build) and operating levies (to operate school facilities.)

Public schools in most sections of the United States are facing severe financial problems. In those states that require voter approval to increase or renew tax levies, the problems are particularly acute.

With frequently faltering national and local economies and cutbacks or eliminations of many federal and state programs of assistance, financing the operation of public schools is becoming an even greater challenge than usual.

Chapter II

The Marketing Concept

The Application of Marketing Tools to Public Schools' Financial Problems

Against this backdrop of the increasing difficulty of gaining public support for school operating levies and bond issues, a new champion is emerging—the use of marketing tools to address and solve public school financing problems.

The art of marketing is not new. It has been around in various forms for many years. The names used to describe this art have been varied and often not accurately descriptive—sales, selling, promotion, merchandising, and so forth. Regardless of the title used, marketing activities have long been associated with products and services produced and sold by profit-making organizations.

During the past two decades, however, the use of marketing and marketing technology has been significantly broadened. Marketing tools have been increasingly applied, and found to be successful, in dealing with situations of a less traditional nature.

Marketing tools have been successfully applied to a variety of nontraditional markets in behalf of nontraditional products such as social services and agencies, political causes, politicians, entertainers, social issues, churches, museums, and schools and school systems.

Marketing Versus Selling

During the past two decades, there has been a significant redefinition of the role, scope, and context of marketing, resulting in the development of an entirely new marketing concept.

Paramount to the broadening and redefining of marketing has been a realization that there is a sharp, distinct difference between marketing and selling.

In essence, this distinction, which is so critical to the development of a marketing approach, identifies selling as "getting rid of what I have," whereas marketing is correctly identified as "having what I can get rid of." Another way of delineating between these two concepts is to understand that selling involves solving the problem of the seller, whereas marketing involves solving the problem of the customer.

This significant distinction between selling and marketing has been a major factor in the reappraisal of the relationship between the major characters in the economic system. Although the distinction of getting rid of what I have and having what I can get rid of may appear to be somewhat glib and possibly mere semantics, the facts prove the opposite. When a firm or organization focuses all its activities upon ridding itself of what it *has*—a product, an inventory, an idea, a set of services, or a physical establishment—by finding a *home* for it somewhere in the marketplace, it all too often has little respect or regard for the actual needs or desires of those who constitute the market. In such situations, there is great likelihood of finding high-pressure activities, much advertising, promotional pressure, and expenditures, and a variety of activities to make the market desire the firm's product.

Such traditional selling is not without success. Over the years, many firms have prospered by developing, producing, and selling the best possible product their resources would allow. The profit (or the realization of an organizational objective) resulting from such activity is unfortunately seen as a function of sales volume. That is, the more sales, the greater the organization's profit or goal realization.

In the modern marketing concept, there is a significant difference in both focus, means or methods used, and objectives to be sought. In this modern concept, focus is on the market—the customer or consumer—and takes into consideration market needs, desires, values, and levels of satisfaction. An attempt is then made to maximize organization objectives (profit, in most cases) by maximizing satisfaction delivered to market members.

The association of profit or organizational objectives realized with satisfactions delivered is distinctly different from the old or traditional sales concept. Instead of focusing internally on the product, marketing focuses externally on consumer satisfaction.

It is with the latter perspective that modern marketing tools may be applied to the situations, problems, and opportunities facing public schools in their efforts to gain and maintain financial as well as other forms of support from their market.

The Tools of Modern Marketing

In order to apply modern marketing tools to the problems of financing facing public schools across this nation, it is important to identify and understand what those tools are.

Those tools (marketing decision variables) that can be brought to bear on situations and problems facing public schools include the following:

1. An identification and analysis of the target market to be served
2. Product development
3. Price development and administration
4. Promotional activity development and administration
5. Physical distribution
6. Follow-up market analysis

Since each of these is incorporated into the details of the following sections of this monograph, a brief introduction to each will be provided in this section.

Identification and analysis of the target market to be served is central to any marketing activity. Before any form of product or mix of satisfaction can be developed for the market, it is essential that the precise segment(s) of the market to be served and the needs, wants, desires, and the current and expected levels of satisfaction of those market segments be determined.

This activity necessarily involves some form of market research. It is at this point that the marketer determines the answers to such questions as follow:

- Who are the members of the market to be served?
- What does that market need?

- How well are those needs being presently met?
- Are there areas in which additional satisfaction can be developed for the market?

For schools, these questions translate into discovering issues critical to determining the acceptance or rejection of operating levies, bond issues, and any form of activity requiring market member (voter) assent. Applying these tools to passage of an operating levy or bond issue passage requires knowledge of major issues as well as nonissues that may exist and identification of beliefs held by voters—whether or not those beliefs are accurate.

It is extremely important for any operating levy or bond issue campaign that identification and accurate evaluation of issues on which a vote might turn be made. Preconceived notions of what issues might be critical tend to be accepted by campaign leadership and dwelled upon in the campaign. Perhaps that evaluation is accurate and actions made based on such an evaluation are adequate, but until market input is solicited, it is dangerous to make any major assumptions and act upon them. It is not only important that any potential issue be identified, but also that the strength of that issue be evaluated. Many times, what appears to loom as a major issue or major campaign strategy proves useless through careful early analysis.

Product development is another tool for developing a successful operating levy or bond issue campaign. From a marketing-oriented position, product is a mix of satisfactions derived from consuming the resources used. In short, the product to be presented to the market is the operating levy or bond issue. Thus, there must be an identification of those satisfactions associated with the passage of a levy or bond issue, that is, what the voters see as benefits. Development of the product cannot proceed until a careful and rigorous analysis of the target market to be reached by an operating levy or bond issue campaign has been made.

Development of a price strategy consistent with the use of modern marketing tools involves establishment of a price that market members must sacrifice in order to gain the satisfaction flowing from the product. Obviously, in the case of an operating levy or bond issue, this price will be reflected in the form of some type of tax. In any marketing-oriented presentation of price, there are numerous considerations, including the establishment of price, its use in conjunction with the values associated with the product, and various means through which that price may be presented to the market.

Development of a promotional strategy, so important to any marketing operation, is no less important when the product is an operating levy or bond issue. It is important that, once again, the needs, desires, and expectations of the market are considered and are an integral part of the promotional materials, activities, and presentation. The area of promotion includes all forms of media and nonmedia advertising, sales presentations, and all public relations, sales promotion, and publicity-related activites.

Development of a physical distribution strategy is likely to be the least readily applicable of any marketing decision variable in such a nonprofit setting as public school financing. It is possible in many such circumstances, however, to incorporate a physical distribution strategy both in the development of the total product to be offered to the market and in a campaign through which that product may be presented. The physical distribution component can be found in determining where to locate a new facility/building and how to distribute (allocate) the benefits from a successful campaign—who gets what in the way of resources from a levy. The political sensitivity of such an issue should be very apparent, and decisions of this nature may be used in structuring the campaign itself. For example, a decision to add additional teachers, specific programs, or facilities at specific buildings or to augment programs related to specific areas within the school district would be a type of physical distribution strategy designating heavier or unique campaign promotion activities in targeted geographic areas.

Follow-up research activities are necessary to assess and monitor the effectiveness of any application of marketing tools, in the traditional profit sector as well as in a nonprofit or service setting. It is only through such procedures that it is possible to know what worked and what didn't, which campaign elements were successful and which were not, which to use in future campaigns and which not to use.

It is important that this assessment be made carefully and quickly after campaign completion so memories of campaign activities and issues are fresh in respondents' memories.

The Role and Position of a Marketing Plan in Addressing Public School Financing Problems

The results from any comprehensive survey and market analysis of community attitudes, positions, and beliefs may become the starting point for efforts at addressing problems the survey revealed.

If there is need to attempt specification (for example, presenting an operating levy or bond issue), the market analysis results should be quickly translated into a precise marketing plan.

The structure of a marketing plan should answer such questions as

- What is to be done (objectives)?
- How is it to be done (strategies and tactics)?
- By whom is it to be done (personnel, organizational structure, and so forth)?
- When is it to be done (the timetable for actions to be taken)?
- What will it cost (the budget)?

Such a plan should be the blueprint for subsequent activities directed toward resolving the problem.

In later sections, the components of the marketing plan (with many suggested tactical activities) are presented and discussed.

Chapter III

Analysis of the Market

Understanding the Market, the Product and the Marketing Campaign

Before the elements of a marketing plan can be developed and combined into a campaign for a specific operating levy or bond issue, it is important that a thorough and accurate understanding of the present community situation (the market) be gained. This must include an understanding of positions, beliefs, attitudes, and perceptions held by people comprising the market—voters or those who might become eligible to vote—and a clear delineation of the problem(s) faced in gaining voter approval of the operating levy/bond issue. Identification of central issues likely to affect the outcome of a campaign is critical, since any effective plan must include provisions to address and promote issues that might stimulate positive votes and to identify (as effectively as possible) issues that might create or reinforce negative votes.

The feeling often exists that issues are known without a specific and structured investigation. Such feelings are frequently erroneous and potentially fatal to a campaign.

To adequately identify and isolate these issues, market analysis research should be performed. Procedures for conducting such an analysis are described in the following section.

The Survey of the Market

Knowledge of the market's (potential consumer's) wants and desires, turn-offs, and "hot and cold buttons" is essential to the effectiveness of any marketing campaign. Marketing a levy or bond issue is no different—the road to a successful campaign begins with an analysis of the attitudes and opinions of potential voters in a community.

To accomplish this analysis, it is necessary to consider and use such procedures as these:

- Selection of the appropriate data-gathering technique (mail survey, phone survey, personal interview)
- Determination of the sample size
- Selection of the sample
- Construction of the data-gathering instrument

Selection of the Appropriate Data-Gathering Technique

There are strengths and weaknesses to any process and awareness of them will aid in selecting the best technique for a given situation.

Mail Survey

The major strengths of mail surveys include time, labor, breadth, and cost. More people can be contacted faster, at a lower cost per contact, and with the least amount of staff when a mail survey is used. The major weaknesses of a mail survey include the rate of return and representativeness of the responses. In most cases, the researcher is fortunate to get a 20 percent return, and these returns may be from people with extreme opinions, either very positive or very negative. Although it is often assumed that assurance of anonymity will result in honest responses, there is no guarantee of this. Lies are extremely difficult to detect in a mail survey.

Contributing to the problem of erroneous information is ambiguity. If a person does not understand the question, there is no one there to provide an explanation. This may result in a wrong answer, no answer, or in the survey being thrown away.

Phone Survey

The major strengths of phone surveys include the depth of response, the ability to clarify ambiguities, and cost. Since there is direct contact with the individual, clarification of responses, reasons, and so forth, can be obtained and questions can be answered. If volunteer help is available and responsive to training, expenses may be minimal.

The major weakness of phone surveys is the representativeness of response. Many people are annoyed at having their daily routines interrupted with phone surveys. As a result, they hang up without responding. Since respondents can "hide" behind their phone's receiver, eye contact cannot be made and the respondent has a greater opportunity to lie. Although a phone survey will traditionally sample only those who have telephone numbers listed in the phone book, this weakness is not as great as it might appear. Those without a telephone cannot normally be contacted, but the loss of contact opportunity due to unlisted numbers may be largely avoided by dialing the three-digit exchange number and then a randomly selected four-digit numeral. (How to use random numbers will be explained in a subsequent section.)

Time is another factor to consider. With volunteers willing to use their home phones or facilities with several phones, a phone survey can be accomplished in a relatively short period of time. If the survey is constructed to take a maximum of five to ten minutes, each volunteer can obtain six to twelve interviews per hour. The time required depends on the number of volunteers and numbers of phones. If only a few volunteers or phones are used, the time needed to complete a phone survey can be considerable.

Personal Interview

The major strengths of interviews are the depth and representativeness of response. Since the interviewer is face to face with the respondent, any ambiguities in the questions can be clarified, and lying is minimized. Even in responding to a personal interview, some respondents will provide deliberately inaccurate answers, but there is less risk of this in a personal interview than in either mail or telephone surveys.

The major weaknesses of personal interviews are time and breadth. Given a limited amount of time, fewer people can be questioned with a personal interview than with the other two techniques.

Expense is another factor to consider. Conducting useful, valid personal interviews requires trained or experienced interviewers. If volunteers with these qualifications cannot be found (and they seldom can be), it is necessary to provide careful training for the interviewers. Do not use untrained interviewers. They can ruin the results of the survey, and their approach could even produce a negative vote on election day.

Deciding which technique to use is complex. If limited resources and few volunteers are available, a mail survey is probably best. With the addition of some volunteers, a phone survey could be considered. Given financial resources and the availability of trained personnel, personal interview is strongly recommended.

Because financial resources and trainable interviewers were available, personal interviews were used by the authors for the marketing of a bond issue in Piqua, Ohio.

Planning the Analysis

Perhaps the most important suggestion is to **start early.** For the best results, planning should begin at least a year in advance. Time is needed to raise funds, obtain volunteers, conduct a maket analysis, analyze its results, and plan campaign strategy.

The authors' planning and development of a bond issue campaign began thirteen months before the election; a market analysis was begun eleven months before the actual election date.

There is a risk in starting a market survey too early. External events could cause a change in public attitudes. If a market analysis is conducted before such an event, the results may be distorted and their use frought with danger. The potential for such a problem occurred in the analysis conducted by the authors prior to the Piqua bond issue campaign.

About two weeks before the planned start of the interviews, it was learned that, due to property reappraisals, most people in the community were going to face a 15 to 20 percent increase in their next tax bills. Unfortunately, the tax bills would not be received until after the scheduled end of the interviewing. There was great concern about the impact such an increase would have on respondents' attitudes and opinions and on the subsequent validity of results. It was decided, therefore, to adjust the interviewing. Half the interviews were conducted before tax bills were sent, and half were conducted afterward. In addition, the latter half of the interviews were spread over a four-week period. These two adjustments permitted assessing the attitude changes before and after tax bills were received and assessing any lasting impact of the reappraisal and a subsequent (unvoted) increase in many respondents' property taxes.

The analyses of the interviews showed a definite negative shift in attitude from the interviews given before receipt of tax bills to the interviews given immediately after receipt of the bills. An interesting and reassuring result was that, in the subsequent three weeks, attitudes shifted back toward a more positive position. By the final week of interviews, there was no difference in responses obtained before and after the mailing of tax bills.

Determination of the Sample Size

For samples to be considered representative of a population, they must be sufficiently large. Too often, conclusions are made from samples that are too small and they result in wrong decisions. The following table provides suggested sample sizes, depending on the size of the population of a community.

Population of Community	Sample Size
1,000-5,000	300-350
5,000-10,000	350-375
10,000-20,000	375-400
over 20,000	400-500

These figures are based on the tables found in *Tables for Statisticians*, Herbert Arfim and Raymond R. Colton, Barnes and Noble College Outline Series, New York (1971).

These sample sizes will have an error factor of about plus or minus 5 percent. In other words, the results of 75 percent yes and 25 percent no were obtained for a survey question. The actual population result would be expected to lie between 70 to 80 percent yes and 20 to 30 percent no.

If it is impossible to obtain the size of the sample indicated, proceed with a smaller sample. In most cases, some information is better than no information. More caution will be needed, however, in the interpretation of the results. Samples less than one hundred are subject to considerable error.

Beware of respondents' refusal to participate. This can signal a negative position on the levy or issue. In the Piqua bond issue study, the school district population equalled approximately twenty-five thousand. It was determined that five hundred people should be interviewed and, perhaps surprisingly, of the 512 contacts necessary to obtain the five hundred interviews, only twelve people refused to be interviewed. In a subsequent section of this chapter, strategies that may have helped create this low refusal rate will be identified and discussed.

Selection of the Sample

The sampling procedure recommended is a proportional, randomized sample. To begin selection of such a sample, voting records of the community, especially the turnout at the most recent elections featuring a school financing issue, are needed. Obtain the total voter turnout for the entire community, and the turnout in each ward, precinct, or township. For example, suppose the community had the following voter turnout:

Ward 1	2,000
Ward 2	1,000
Ward 3	500
Ward 4	500
Township A	1,000
Total Turnout	5,000

Ward 1 had a 2,000 voter turnout out of a total community turnout of 5,000; its proportion of the total vote was 2,000/5,000 (40 percent). Likewise, Ward 2 had a proportion of 1,000/5,000 (20 percent). Wards 3 and 4 each had 500/5,000

(10 percent), and Township A had 1,000/5,000 (20 percent).

Let us suppose that a sample of four hundred people is needed for the survey. When this sample is selected, 40 percent or 160 people should be selected from Ward 1; 20 percent, or eighty people, should be selected from Ward 2; 10 percent, or forty people, should be selected from Ward 3; 10 percent, or forty people, should be selected from Ward 4; and 20 percent, or eighty people, should be selected from Township A.

Once the number of people needed from each political subdivision is determined, a table of random numbers should be used. Such tables, found in most statistics texts, ensure that every member of the population has a known chance of inclusion in the sample.

Next, obtain a street map for each ward and township and list and number all streets in each given political subdivision. For example, suppose Ward 1, above, has fifty streets. List the streets and number them from 1-50. As a recommended procedure, pick about one-fourth of the streets from the sample. In the case of Ward 1, this would be about thirteen streets.

Now, turn to the table of random numbers, consisting of columns of numerals. Since, in the case of Ward 1 only two-digit numerals will be used to number the streets one to fifty, only two-digit numerals will be used from the table. Typically, either the first two digits or the last two digits of the numerals would be selected. Start anywhere in the table, but do not start at the same place every time a different sample is selected.

For example, suppose the first two digits of the starting numeral in the table are two-one. Street number twenty-one, therefore, would be selected for the sample. Continue reading down the column, using the first two digits of each numeral. If a two-digit numeral occurs that exceeds the numbering needed (in this case, fifty), skip it. If a two-digit numeral occurs that has already been used, skip it.

Since thirteen streets are to be selected for Ward 1, the process is continued until all these streets are chosen.

Now that the streets are selected, it is necessary to determine the number of homes to choose from each. It is important here to know the relative number of homes on each of the streets selected. A street index listing all the homes is helpful. From this index, count the total number of homes, determine the proportion of homes represented by each street, and use that proportion to select the appropriate number. For example, if there are three hundred homes on the thirteen streets selected from Ward 1, and street A has thirty homes, 30/300 equals 10 percent of the sample homes will be selected from street A.

Recall that 160 people were to be selected from Ward 1. Therefore, 10 percent of 160 equals sixteen homes from street A. If street B has fifteen homes, 15/300 equals 5 percent; 5 percent of 160 equals eight homes from street B. Repeat this process for each of the streets.

Much work can be avoided in this step if someone knows the relative proportions of the number of homes on these streets. Thus, if it is known that street A has about 10 to 15 percent of the homes, use this figure to obtain the needed number for the sample. As long as the knowledge is trustworthy, the estimates will be close and much time and energy will be saved. Count each individual apartment in a complex as a home.

With the number of homes determined, the only remaining step is to select specific homes. The technically correct way to do this is to number the homes on each street from 1-N (N equals the total number of homes) and use the table of random numbers. To select the sixteen homes on street A, the homes would be numbered from one to thirty, and the table of random numbers would be used to pick the sixteen houses. Such a method is recommeded if those doing the interviewing are familiar with the neighborhoods. Otherwise, they might pick homes of people they know. If the observers are not familiar with the neighborhood, and it is strongly suggested that they not be in order to avoid bias, the interviewers should be instructed to divide the interviews evenly between both sides of the street and evenly between blocks. This avoids taking time to number streets and using the table of random numbers in the last step.

While all this may seem complex and cumbersome on initial reading, a little practice will show how easy it really is. This procedure is necessary to allow a representative population sample to be considered. To simply pick a street may consciously or unconsciously bias the outcome of a survey.

In summary, the steps in selecting a sample are as follows:

1. Use the table on page 13 to determine the size of the sample
2. Determine the number of people needed in each political subdivision by using the proportion based on past voter turnout
3. Use a table of random numbers to select the streets to be involved in the survey
4. Determine the number of homes to be surveyed on each street by using the proportion based on total number of homes on the streets

One final suggestion may save time when specific homes have been selected using the table of random numbers. Technically, if no one is home, the interviewer should return at another time, but to save time, the interviewer could choose the home next door.

Construction of the Data-Gathering Instrument

Formulating Hypotheses

A good data-gathering instrument does not appear out of the blue—it is based on testing preestablished concerns and questions, or hypotheses. What relationships should be tested? What factors can produce negative attitudes toward a levy or bond issue? What factors can produce positive attitudes? What demographic (age, sex, race, and so forth) characteristics should be determined; how do these relate to attitudes?

A group of researchable hypotheses generated from several meetings with Piqua community leaders are listed below. There are two reasons for providing this list: (1) to provide hypotheses that might be tested in other communities; and (2) to show how these hypotheses are reflected in the instrument developed for Piqua.

Hypotheses

1. Economics is a major factor--perhaps both positively and negatively
2. People do not want to pay more taxes
3. It is cheaper to build now than later
4. People have pride in their community and want to offer their children what other neighboring communities offer
5. Catholic voters are not supportive of public school financial issues (Piqua has a large Catholic population attending parochial schools)
6. The older the voter, the more negatively inclined the voter
7. There is a difference in attitude between registered and unregistered voters
8. The site of the new school is a major factor in voter attitude (in this case the land was to be donated, but the site was not central to the town)
9. There is concern over the intended use of the old high school
10. Perceived frills added to the new high school are a negative factor to some voters
11. The school board is perceived as credible and, therefore, is not a negative factor
12. Availability of a model and interior plans for the school is a positive factor
13. Loss of North Central Accreditation is a factor in affecting people's attitudes (the loss in Piqua was due to the physical condition of the old high school.)

Preparing Questionnaires and Interviews

Once hypotheses are formulated and the necessary demographic information is determined, the bases are established for questions to be included in an interview or questionnaire. While this section is not intended to be a textbook on survey instrument construction, there are several suggestions that may be of benefit.

1. *The method of responding should allow for brevity.*
Whether by phone, personal interview, or mail, a better rate of return is obtained and there is less difficulty recording answers when respondents have been provided with a quick, convenient way of answering. The easiest way to do this is to develop questions requiring the respondent to choose one of several alternatives. These *forced-choice* types of items could include

a. Attitudinal statements, to which the respondents indicate their feelings by choosing "Strongly agree," "Agree," "Undecided," "Disagree," or "Strongly disagree." For examples of this type of item, see the copy of the instrument in Appendix A, Items 1-6. A variation eliminates the undecided category and forces the respondent to be positive or negative. The choices for this alternative are "Strongly agree," "Agree," "Slightly agree," "Slightly disagree," "Disagree," and "Strongly disagree." If the degree of agreement is not important and you feel either of these two alternatives provides too much discrimination, you might want to offer only three choices—"Agree," "Undecided," and "Disagree" (see Items 53-58).

b. Multiple choice items, in which the respondents choose the alternative that best fits their opinion or attitude. Questions 19-26 and 50-52 are examples of this type. This is a good technique for obtaining demographic information (see Items 81-102).

c. Rating items, in which the respondent is given a list of choices to rate according to degree of importance; for example, "Very important," "Somewhat important," or "Not important." Such items are very useful in their potential to influence voting. Examples of this type are Items 27-45 and 59-75.

d. Ranking items in which the respondents order their preferences from highest to lowest. An abbreviated variation of this procedure asks them to pick their top few or bottom few choices. Examples of this type are Items 46-49 and 76-79.

Although this list is not intended to be exhaustive, these are the item types the authors have found most useful and adaptable to any of the three alternative survey procedures discussed. The initial information on the Piqua bond issue was obtained through personal interviews, but phone or mail surveys could have posed many of the same questions.

Notice that in each item type above, respondent answers were brief. Respondents did not have to take time to compose answers as they would with open-ended questions. Remember that the function of an up-front market survey is to test hypotheses and to have respondents react to them.

Open-ended questions also lack comprehensiveness. Given a fixed amount of time, more topics and ideas can be covered with forced-choice items than with open-ended items. There were many hypotheses to test, and open-ended questions would have taken too much time for respondents to answer and for the interviewers to record and analyze.

2. *The total time to respond to the instrument should be as short as possible.* One way to guarantee a poor response rate is to have an instrument that takes a long time to complete. This is crucial in a mail survey, since there is no opportunity to interact with the respondent. Any questionnaire that takes over ten to fifteen minutes to complete risks becoming a one-handed, fade-away jump shot into the waste basket, making forced-choice questions better than open-ended questions in a mail survey. People are much more willing to make check marks than they are to write sentences or paragraphs.

Total response time must also be seriously considered with phone surveys and personal interviews. People may become irritated and impatient and hang up during a long phone interview. The same can also occur with a personal interview. It is important to remember that interviewers are intruding into an individual's private life and that respondents are doing a favor by granting some of their time.

There was some concern about the length of the Piqua interview after its initial development. It looked long, but after trying it out, we determined it could be completed in fifteen to twenty minutes, which is not too long for a personal interview (we recommend that a personal interview not exceed twenty-five minutes). For phone surveys, a maximum of ten minutes is recommended.

3. *Assure the respondents of anonymity.*
In most cases, there should be little need to obtain the respondent's name. Assuring anonymity enhances the obtaining of honest information. In the directions to the respondent, whether by phone, mail, or personal interview, state that names will not be used. In fact, don't even ask for names. The respondents should feel free to answer as they feel, not as they think they are supposed to feel (see the directions at the beginning of the interview in Appendix A).

4. *Avoid very personal or threatening questions.*
Even though anonymity is assured, the respondent is placed in an uncomfortable position when asked very personal or threatening questions; for example, "Have any of your children been suspended from school?" or "How much income do you earn?" Such questions make the individual hesitant to respond honestly not only to these but also to questions that follow and may also lead them to refuse to cooperate. If such questions are asked in a phone survey, respondents may hang up, and if they occur in a mail survey, it probably won't be returned. In surveys designated to establish the attitudes of a community toward a financial issue, these types of questions should be unnecessary.

If it is felt that a personal question is absolutely necessary, two techniques can be used to make questions more palatable to respondents. The first technique immediately precedes a personal question with a very simple, innocuous one. An example of this is found in Items 100 and 101 of the Piqua survey. Because it was hypothesized that religion might be a factor in the voting outcome and that, for some, asking their religious preference is a very personal question, it was preceded by a question asking where they bought their groceries.

The second technique provides respondents with a series of choices enabling them to avoid considering themselves either extremely low or extremely high. For example, a question asking for the amount of education respondents have might make them feel very uncomfortable if theirs is the lowest category listed. Therefore, they may be given one or more categories that they can put themselves above, e.g., "No schooling," "Through third grade," "Through elementary school," "Through junior high," and so forth.

Age is another very personal area to some. Note in Question 84 of the Piqua survey that four very broad categories were provided. Respondents did not have to reveal their exact age or place themselves in extremely narrow categories.

5. *Don't jeopardize response accuracy by backing respondents into a corner.*
Responses tend to be inflated positively by asking such questions as "How do you plan to vote on the upcoming levy?" This was verified by asking the Piqua sample how they voted in the last bond issue election. Not surprisingly, responses were about 67 percent for and 33 percent against, yet the bond issue failed by 60 percent to 40 percent. This question was asked, however, to lead into a question of much greater importance—how they would vote this time?

A much more accurate projection of voting outcomes can be gained by allowing respondents to choose from such responses as "I'd certainly vote for," "I'd almost certainly vote for," "I might vote for," "I'm uncertain," "I might vote against," "I'd almost certainly vote against," "I'd certainly vote against," and so forth. As we will show, a more accurate and useful projection can result using this less restrictive form of response.

6. *Provide a scapegoat to increase accuracy.*
When asking a how-do-you-plan-to-vote question, a scapegoat giving respondents a socially acceptable factor to blame for their negative feelings may increase response accuracy.

The scapegoat used in the Piqua study was property value reappraisal. In surveys conducted prior to the mailing of the semiannual tax bills, the following question was used:

"Miami County property has been reappraised recently, and when you receive your next bill, you will likely find that your property taxes are somewhat higher. Suppose that you find that your property taxes are 15 to 20 percent higher as a result of the reappraisal. Would this have any effect on how you would vote on a bond issue for a new high school?"

a. *No effect*, I'd still certainly vote for it.
b. *Unlikely*, I'd probably still vote for it.
c. *Likely* to cause me to vote against a new high school.
d. *Certain* to cause me to vote against a new high school.

Allowing respondents to place the blame on property tax increase through reappraisal gave what was considered a more accurate indication of the community's likelihood of voting for the bond issue. As shown in a subsequent section, the prediction of the voting outcome was based on this question.Even if a community has not had a recent reappraisal, a question making property tax the scapegoat could still be constructed. For example, "Considering the amount of property tax you currently pay, how likely is the amount to influence your vote on the upcoming school levy?"

Another good alternative to use when it is difficult to find a logical scapegoat is a projective technique. Instead of asking respondents how they would vote, they are asked how they think their neighbors would vote. The assumption is that they will project their own feelings onto their neighbors and, therefore, will really indicate how they personally feel.

7. *Publicize the survey.*
Greater return rates are usually obtained when surveys are publicized in advance. An announcement in the newspaper or on local radio or television stations emphasizing the importance of a response, the importance of data representativeness, and respondent anonymity is usually sufficient. Survey dates and times should also be announced.

People tend to be more receptive with this advance publicity. It is common for surveyors to be greeted with such comments as "We've been expecting you," "I've heard about this," or "Oh good! We're one of the sample!"

8. *Test survey questions in advance.*
This suggestion is crucial to the success of any survey. Whether a mail survey, a phone interview, or a personal interview, do not administer an untested questionnaire to the sample. The testing phase uncovers ambiguities and biases and pinpoints the need to omit or add questions.

A small sample (ten or twelve) is needed for testing a questionnaire. (Note, they should not be a part of the final survey sample.) Questions are administered under conditions similar to the actual study, that is, they are read aloud if a phone survey or personal interview is planned. Have the volunteers read the survey and mark it if a mail survey is planned.

After the survey is completed, discuss each question with respondents, focusing on ambiguities, terminology, clarity, ease of response, appropriateness of alternative choices, bias, unnecessary questions, and questions that should be added.

Questionnaire testing may also be done using interested parties, such as school board members, teachers, and parents, but must *never* be used to replace testing with a consumer/voter sample at large—only to supplement it.

Once the testing is done, make necessary revisions, retest the revisions, and prepare the final draft of the instrument.

Projecting Voting Outcomes from Results of a Market Research Study

On sensitive issues (in contrast to candidate elections), respondents questioned on their voting intentions tend to give socially acceptable answers. Thus, actual responses must be adjusted for such a tendency and any projections of likely voting outcomes must reflect this phenomena.

It has been the authors' experience that in making projections of voting outcomes from surveys giving respondents a scapegoat and choices ranging from "Certainly vote for" to "Certainly vote against," it is necessary to adjust along the following lines. Actual positive votes can be considered as coming from *not more than*

- 90% of those who claim they will *certainly vote for* an issue
- 60% of those who claim they will *almost certainly vote for* an issue
- 30% of those who claim they *might vote for* an issue
- 10% of those who claim to be *really uncertain*

Projections are valid as of the precise date(s) of the survey only and do not have the benefit of any campaign effort. It has been the authors' experience that effective campaign efforts add from 4 to 18 percent more positive votes to the precampaign projection.

Chapter IV

The Organizational Structure and Major Strategic Decision Areas

Organizational Structure and Duties for the Operating Levy or Bond Issue Campaign

The key to any successful campaign is the organization preceding it and accompanying it to completion. An organizational outline for the structure of such a campaign follows on page 25.

Note that the organizational outline calls for the following:

I. *Steering Committee.* This committee should consist of but not be limited to
   A. The campaign cochairs (or single chair)
   B. The campaign coordinator (optional)
   C. Representation from each of the following:
      1. Chamber of commerce
      2. Board of education
      3. Administration of public schools
      4. Teachers from public schools
   D. Other members may be added to the steering committee at the discretion of and on the majority vote of the steering committee.

II. *Campaign Chair* (or cochair). This extremely important position must be filled with a visible, capable, dedicated, competent person (or people) who has a schedule flexible enough to allow participation in the full range of leadership activities demanded as the campaign progresses. If there are cochairs, at least one should be female.

   All campaign-related announcements, decisions, and information should come through the chair. The day-to-day direction of the campaign rests here. Primary areas of direct involvement include recruitment, training, directing, and coordinating all volunteer worker activities; development of the campaign theme and/or slogan; development of a campaign advertising plan; development of a campaign brochure; selection of all advertising copy to be used in the media; scheduling and placing of all advertising; scheduling and coordination of all nonadvertising promotional activities; management of publicity campaign-related news releases and feature stories; appointment by campaign cabinet members; and chairing the steering committee and campaign cabinet. This list emhasizes the prudence of selecting cochairs.

III. *Treasurer of the Campaign.* The responsibilities of this position shall be to record all transactions, approve all expenditures (in conference with the campaign chair(s), sign checks related to the campaign, and to complete all reports and forms required by election laws.

IV. *Campaign Coordinator* (optional). A position of campaign coordinator may be created to use outside, professional assistance in advising and consulting with the campaign chair(s). Arrangements for such a position should be made by any organization (chamber of commerce, manufacturer's association, and so forth) financing the campaign.

V. *Campaign Cabinet.* This group shall consist of the campaign chair(s) (who shall preside), the campaign coordinator (if used), the chair of each of the divisions, and any other members of the steering committee designated by that committee or appointed by the campaign chair. The overall guidance of the campaign will be under the control of the campaign cabinet.

VI. *Chair of the Residential Division.* This person, possibly the single most important subcommittee chair, has leaders for each of the wards and the townships. Each ward or township leader needs coordinators for each precinct or neighborhood, and each of these should have a series of block captains. Each of the captains is responsible for aiding in recruiting and directing a group of two to five volunteer workers.

Foremost in the plans for organization of the campaign is an effort to reach systematically into every residential neighborhood, every block, and every rural neighborhood within the school district. To accomplish this, a large number of volunteers (perhaps several hundred) is needed. Recruiting and carefully training and motivating this group is a first priority following the establishment of the top-level campaign leadership.

It is the responsibility of the residential division to assure that

A. Prior to the deadline for voter registration, each block or neighborhood volunteer determines, through visitation, the general inclination of each adult household member in his or her designated area. The volunteer should then compile a list of those likely to vote for the levy and indicating whether such people are registered. (This activity is discussed in greater detail in a later section.)

B. Prior to election day, each volunteer delivers a campaign brochure to the households in his or her district and provides answers to any questions raised.

C. Prior to the deadline for filing an application for an absentee ballot, the volunteers assist in arranging the absentee ballot voting of any positively inclined household member(s) in his or her area—shut-ins, college students, service personnel, and so forth.

D. On election day or the previous day, each person identified as favorable to the issue is contacted by phone or by personal visit and is urged to vote. Note: Separate ad hoc groups should be formed to specifically assist in telephone reminders and voter transportation, including such activities as babysitting for voters.

VII. *Chair of the Manufacturing Division.* This division interacts with two groups of voters and potential vote influencers—manufacturing employers and employees. Activities directed at each of these groups will be coordinated by a respective group chair, as follows:

A. Chair for Manufacturing Employers. This person should be a well-known and respected industrialist. Responsibilities include obtaining endorsements and public support, willingness to participate in newspaper and radio ads, and writing letters to the editor.

B. Chair for Manufacturing Employees. This person should be a respected union person who can see and show the value of an effective public school system to organized labor groups. Responsibilities include coordinating promotional activities within each plant, factory, or unionized facility and attempting to gain the union's endorsement of the levy (at least informally).

VIII. *Chair of the Business/Professional Division.* The chair of this division obtains the endorsement and active support of the following segments of the community:

A. Business leaders—retail, service, and so forth

B. Professional leaders—legal, clergy, medical, political leaders, and so forth.

IX. *Chair of the Special Events and Promotions Division.* This person is responsible for such ad hoc activities as parades, and celebrity and community events.

The Structure of an Organization to Campaign for a Levy or Bond Issue

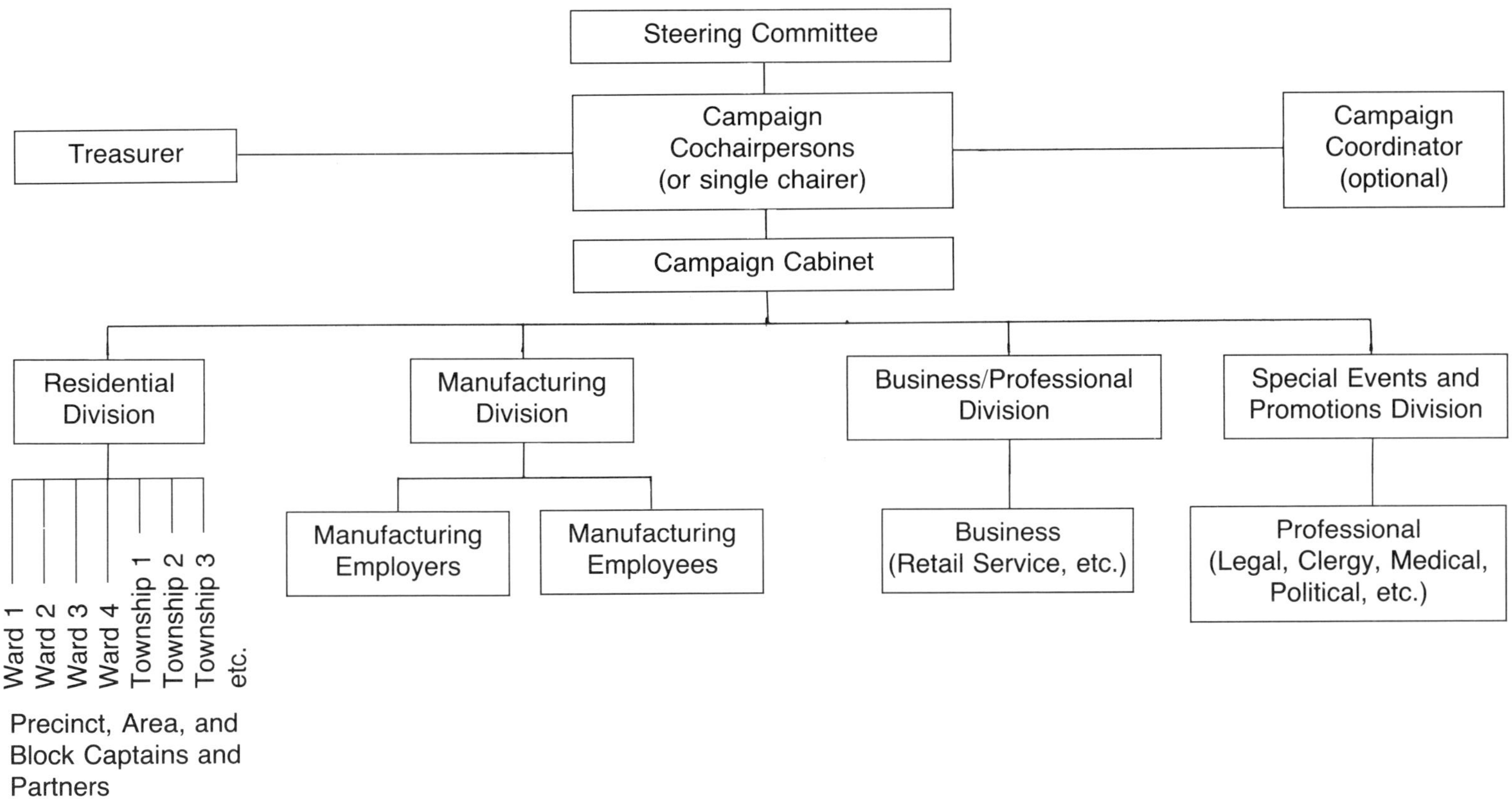

Chapter V

Developing the Strategy and Tactics of an Effective Campaign

Timing Requirements for an Effective Campaign

A successful operating levy or bond issue campaign depends on a timetable and a detailed planning calender. One of the most frequent, self-inflicted problems school campaign organizations encounter is insufficient time to develop an effective campaign.

The actual planning of the campaign should be initiated months in advance of the media campaign, making the period of several weeks just prior to an election, when media advertising is running, the frosting on the cake.

The campaign operation may require as much as one year of lead time prior to an election date, depending upon the steps to be included. It is important to remember that adequate time must be allowed for development of both the design and the implementation of such a research project. Because conditions could change between the time the research was done and the time of the election, it is important to reiterate that any local economic, political, or social developments be anticipated as far ahead as possible.

Even when no market research is done prior to an election, it is necessary that campaign organization be developed several months in advance. It has been the authors' experience that firm organizational structure should be developed approximately six months prior to the date of an election. This time frame ensures the best chances of success and avoids disaster.

The amount of time devoted to the actual campaign for an operating levy or bond issue will be much shorter. Since resources for media advertising and other promotional activities and events are normally quite limited, it is important that the actual campaign not begin too soon. Experience teaches that a period of two to three weeks is adequate for the presentation of an actual media campaign.

Target Market Identification
The Selected Voter Registration Market

Nowhere is the importance of careful market analysis any greater than in the determining of various segments of the target market to be addressed. The most significant result of the initial market analysis conducted by the authors in the Piqua school district may have been the determination that, of the respondents who were not registered to vote, over 70 percent had a negative attitude toward the bond issue. Had it been assumed, as it is often, that a mass voter registration campaign would be beneficial to passage of the issue/levy, the campaign would have contributed to a defeat. This finding and the resulting strategy probably made the time and resources expended on an up-front market analysis worthwhile.

Armed with this significant information, it was imperative that any voter registration campaign be conducted on a selective basis, using what might be considered a *rifle* rather than a *shotgun* approach. Where such a research finding is available—the unregistered voter is not typically an automatically positive voter—the role of this segment of a target market becomes critical.

In most states, voters must commonly be registered by a specific date prior to the election. In Ohio, for example, the registration period closes thirty days prior to election day, and any registration activities had to be conducted with that time frame in mind. Since much organization and training is necessary before any voter registration campaign can be conducted, it is imperative that a lengthy lead time be established. We suggest the voter registration campaign start a minimum of four months before the election to allow adequate time for the recruiting and training of volunteers (a small army of volunteers is highly recommended) and the carrying out of actual voter registration assignments. Training ensures a consistent approach by volunteers and provides a good opportunity for the volunteers to ask questions.

With the knowledge that every previously unregistered (but positive) voter who is registered and brought to the polls represents a brand new positive vote, the undertaking of a selective, low-key voter registration campaign can proceed. Since there is the potential to reach and register a large number of positive voters, the commitment of time and volunteer effort is essential.

In order to adequately cover the market (city, townships, voting areas, and so forth), a large number of volunteers must be recruited. Volunteers may be previous election campaign workers, interested parents who are or have been active in school organizations and activities, teachers, or other school staff members. If certain teachers or administrative personnel are quite unpopular in the community, their involvement can be dangerous, but the advantage of using well-educated and qualified teachers and professional staff is likely to outweigh any disadvantages.

Among the alternative strategies for reaching unregistered, positive voters, the "packaging" of residences in the school district proved very successful to the authors. Separate lists of a designated number of households (ten to twelve, as a typical example) are compiled and the separate lists used as the assigned territories for each volunteer in the preregistration campaign. Volunteer workers are most effective when working in their own neighborhoods or with acquaintances.

Volunteers select a packet or list of residential areas adjacent to their homes and assume responsibility for all eligible voters within each residence.

Responsibilities fall into two time frames. During the first, prior to the close of the voter registration (from sixty to ninety days prior to the actual election), volunteers contact each household on their list and attempt, as unobtrusively as possible, to raise questions and discuss issues related to the upcoming operating levy or bond issue. The purpose of the discussion is to determine how each eligible adult resident would vote on the levy or bond issue. A number of rather bland statements can be used to make this determination, such as the statement "I will be the neighborhood resource person this fall when the operating levy/bond issue campaign is conducted. Are there any questions you would like to ask or any information I can get for you?"*

Such questions and comments trigger responses from residents, allowing astute volunteers to make a rather precise judgment regarding respondents' inclinations. Volunteers must pinpoint positive and negative voters *without* campaigning or arguing with any respondent.

Before visiting, volunteers should be encouraged to check appropriate voter registration lists to determine the registration status of respondents. Once a volunteer

*For a complete script, see Appendix B.

determines that a respondent is a positive voter but is not presently registered, the opportunity to register a brand new positive voter presents itself.

From the contacts made in the neighborhood before the close of voter registration, the volunteer should compile two separate lists. The first list includes registered, and identified as likely positive, voters. This list also includes each voter's name, address, and precinct and ward (or township) of residence. This list is then used in a variety of ways (discussed in subsequent sections) during the campaign and on election day to assure the best possible turnout of positive voters. The second list includes likely positive voters who are currently not registered to vote.

Each volunteer worker assumes the responsibility of changing unregistered but positive voters into registered voters. In many areas, volunteer workers can carry voter registration materials with them and register voters on the spot. This method is effective, because it ensures follow-through by respondents and allows volunteers to assist in an accurate registration process and to expedite the return of forms. In other areas, it is necessary to take the prospective voter to a board of elections, post office, library, or other designated location. Once the registration is completed, the volunteer adds this person's name to the list of positive registered voters.

It is impossible to overstate the importance of this procedure. The thrill of identifying and registering a positive voter is a boost not only to the campaign but also to the morale of the volunteer. In effect, volunteers add one vote to their own personal voting capability each time they add a positive voter. Success stories should be shared with members of the campaign organization through bulletins, newsletters, and so forth. Success does breed success.

If the entire market area is blanketed with volunteers making personal contacts, nearly all voters and their inclinations (positive or negative), and all potentially positive unregistered voters can be identified. It is idealistic, however, to assume that an entire market area can be covered with this procedure. The most significant limitation to total market coverage is the lack of adequate volunteers. If each volunteer, for example, is being asked to call on ten or twelve residences, the group of volunteers necessary will be approximately 8 to 10 percent of the entire population of the area. In most communities, it is difficult to find such a large army of volunteers, meaning that either some areas of the market will be left uncontacted by the preregistration campaign deadline or that many volunteers will be asked to accept greater responsibility. It is not unusual that some volunteers—particularly after turning unregistered positive voters into registered voters—will be so enthused that they will devote considerably more time to the project than they had originally anticipated. It is common to find some volunteers who will accept not one packet of residential households (ten to twelve residences), but two, three, or more. When this happens, the proportion of market coverage increases dramatically. It is also true, however, that the intention of keeping volunteer workers active within their neighborhoods is violated, but this is a small price to pay for gaining additional volunteer coverage.

Generally, if as much as 75 to 80 percent of an entire market area can be covered, a significant number of previously unregistered, positive voters will be identified.

Reaching and Registering Voters Who can Assist Without Paying Taxes

The importance of reaching positive, unregistered voters has been stressed. A unique segment of this group in most communities greatly increases the potential for success of the operating levy or bond issue.

A substantially growing segment of renters—especially those renting space in an apartment complex or senior citizen's facility—pay rent in the form of a fixed proportion of their income, regardless of their circumstances. Whether they are employed, retired, or receiving Social Security or government assistance, the federal government's role in providing rent subsidies for those on a fixed or limited income is increasing. *This distinction is of enormous importance to campaign leadership.*

Property tax increases are paid directly by property owners, so they are more sensitive to tax increases. But they are also indirectly paid by renters. The authors' research indicates that renters are more likely to vote for an operating levy than property owners, because they typically pay property tax increases indirectly in the form of increased rental payments. Where individuals simply spend a proportion of income for rent, *a property tax increase is not felt either directly or indirectly.* Hundreds, even thousands, of people of voting age will therefore pay no additional tax or higher rent as the result of local property tax increase to support an operating levy or bond issue. These individuals can mean the difference between winning and losing an election.

The most difficult part of presenting a request for support of an operating levy or bond issue is encountering the reluctance to pay higher property taxes, higher rent, or higher payments in any form. It is refreshing and enormously productive to be able to address a segment of voters, like those identified in the preceeding paragraphs, with the absolute statement that "You can support the schools, kids, etc., and it will not cost you a dime to do so." This profound statement can be made honestly, openly, and enthusiastically to renters whose payments are made in the form of a proportion of income. To such individuals, an increase in property taxes is indeed meaningless.

Another exciting aspect of this market segment is the typically low level of voter registration and participation. Even those registered are less likely to vote. Indeed, many such people have never voted in their lives.

It is impossible to overstate the importance of reaching these people before the voter registration deadline. It is likely that a door-to-door canvas of such neighborhoods or apartment complexes will reveal that as many as 90 to 95 percent of residents are not registered. It is not difficult to register these people if the procedure is adequately explained and made sufficiently painless. The authors have found that liberalized voter registration rules frequently make it possible for campaign leaders to carry registration materials with them and to register such people upon first contact.

There are several ground rules for addressing this significant voter segment. It is important that residents be involved and included in voter registration efforts. Ideally, a two-person operation should take place—a member of the campaign organization and a local resident should work together in conducting a voter registration campaign. This makes potential registrants more comfortable and opens the door for an explanation of the need for a levy or bond issue.

To avoid confusion and to save time, the actual completion of forms should be handled by the campaign worker. Most forms simply request name, address, date of birth, place of birth, perhaps former residence, and the signature of the person applying for registration. If the campaign worker will simply solicit that information from the registrant, then allow the registrant to review the document or documents and sign in the appropriate places, the process can be expedited. Typically there are two cards requesting similar information to complete in order to register a person. It is assumed that the conversation between the campaign worker, the local resident, and the person being called upon will ascertain whether or not the person (1) is aware of the upcoming operating levy or bond issue; (2) realizes they have an opportunity to support the youth of the community (often their own young people and children); and, (3) understands that it will cost them nothing. From experience, the authors can attest that individuals are highly cooperative. The opportunity to assist others at no cost to themselves is a combination that very few people will turn down.

Simply registering such previously unregistered and positive voters, however, is not sufficient. A concerted, coordinated, and carefully controlled effort must be made to bring these people to the polls on election day.

In summary, contacting such people, bringing along a local resident for identification, gaining entrance and cooperation, assisting in completing the registration forms, and then returning the registration forms to the board of elections, library, or other designated place, coupled with follow-up on election day, will produce a genuine and significant outpouring of positive votes. This area of the campaign alone can turn many close elections in favor of the campaign organization.

Registering High School and College Students and Those in Military Services

In conducting voter registration, do not overlook a potentially significant group—students. Many high school students will be of voting age and should be contacted. It is best to use a group of student volunteers for this task.

In addition to high school students, college students also comprise a pool of voters who require attention. A committee of volunteers should identify those who are still at home, or will be home at the time of the election, and those who are or will be away at college when the election occurs. Not only can those who are currently living at home be registered, but registration materials can also be sent to those who are away. In a cover letter to these students, it should be indicated that absentee ballots can be requested. Enclose an application for an absentee ballot.

Just as with the other registration effort, volunteers contacting college students or military personnel must carefully screen the list and include only those thought to be favorable toward the issue. To do this, it is best to use people from each of the past five years' graduating classes as a screening committee and as contacts. The contact itself—together with a request for cooperation, support, and admonitions to register and vote by absentee ballot—should then be initiated by the committee members. The request and influence by peers is more likely to cause a favorable response.

Careful follow-up is required. Student-committee members must follow up on election day to make certain newly registered high school students get to the polls. Since voting has not been a part of their normal pattern, they must be given special care. The follow-up task is somewhat different for college students and young people in military service. After a committee of peers has identified those positive-leaning people and they have been sent materials for registration and absentee ballots, it is important that several stages of follow-up be initiated. Include a stamped envelope addressed to campaign committee headquarters so registration materials and requests for absentee ballots can be received by the screening committee rather than sent to the local board of elections. In this way, the committee can check off the names of those who have completed registration or requested absentee ballots before forwarding the materials to the board of elections. People who have not responded should then be recontacted while sufficient time exists prior to registration deadline.

All those responding to either the initial contact or subsequent follow-up efforts must then be contacted approximately ten days prior to election to complete and mail their absentee ballots. It may be possible to inspect records at the board of elections a few days prior to election to determine who of those contacted have not yet returned absentee ballots. Further contact by phone or through friends or family members may add quite a number of additional positive votes via absentee ballot. This phase of the follow-up operation requires careful organization and considerable effort, but it can be highly successful and rewarding. There is great satisfaction in seeing an absentee ballot arrive, knowing that it comes from a positive voter and knowing that the committee's efforts have made it happen. In a close election, it is just such frequently overlooked or poorly coordinated activities such as this that can mean the difference.

Development of a Name for the Campaign Organization

Any organization that confronts a critical problem in the community, such as the passage of an operating levy or bond issue, needs as much visability and easy identification as possible. For this reason, a name should be chosen very early in the planning process. The name chosen, often an acronym, should indicate both the identity of the area to be served and, if possible, the objective of the organization itself. For example, in the campaign planned for the community of Piqua, Ohio, the organization was known as Piqua's Active School Supporters (PASS). The fact that the campaign was to be waged in the fall—during football season—was relevant in the selection of the name. More meaningful, however, was the identification of the group's intentions.

Development of a Campaign Theme

A theme may become the rallying cry for all that is done in behalf of the campaign. The theme should be consistent with the objectives of the campaign—to pass an operating levy or bond issue, to support the schools, and so forth. The theme may also indicate the desired action of the voters—the casting of a positive vote, acceptance of responsibilities in the community, and so forth. For this reason, it is strongly recommended that the campaign leadership brainstorm to identify possible themes for the campaign. The themes "This is the Year," "It's Time to Take a Stand," "It's Up to Us," (or, "It's *Still* Up to Us," used as a follow-up to an earlier unsuccessful campaign) were employed.

Development for each of the themes noted above required a specific area of reasoning. The theme, "This is the Year," was directed toward passage of a bond issue that had already been rejected several times. The campaign committee hoped to develop a feeling of resolution in the market/voters by emphasizing the word *this*, to convince voters that the time had come to make the positive decision.

The theme, "It's Time to Take a Stand," reflects a similar commitment. This theme was most frequently and effectively coupled with media promotions identifying people who had previously voted against the issue but who were now convinced there was adequate reason to support it.

The theme "It's Up to Us" attempted to emphasize the acceptance of responsibility at the local level. Campaign materials addressed the relative decline of state and federal contributions and the relative proportional increase in total funding provided by local taxes.

When voters failed to respond to this appeal, a follow-up campaign conducted three months later used the theme "It's *Still* Up to Us," insisting that the responsibility *still* rested increasingly with local taxpayers.

We are not suggesting that any one of these themes will apply to every situation a local district faces, but that the development of a theme can, and should, reflect the circumstances and situations individual to the community and campaign. There is no cure-all theme or slogan, and the development of either depends on the creativity of the campaign leadership.

Nonschool Funding and Involvement

If a bond issue or operating levy campaign is to be successful, the need for outside funding and involvement is imperative. In many states, campaigns must be funded without school monies. As a result, it is standard practice to ask local manufacturers, financial institutions, and other business and industrial concerns to donate money for the campaign. Solicitations are often time consuming, however, and may require a small army of volunteers. The local chamber of commerce can expedite these efforts, if its chief officer has a good working relationship with the school system, by soliciting chamber members for the funding and running of the campaign.

For the authors, the local chamber of commerce was one of the first and earliest contacts made. Their support was invaluable, not only financially, but also in providing campaign leadership and design. Many of the members are highly visible and respected in the community, and their endorsement can gain positive votes.

Their expertise in organization and advertising and their spirit of community involvement are resources waiting to be tapped. If chamber support can be gained, volunteers are freed to search for positive voters.

Each community has different resources they can tap for campaign funding, but the tapping must be done and must be done early. In addition to the chamber, other agencies should be contacted, including service clubs and fraternal organizations whose very objectives are to meet the needs of community youth. Most organizations interested in helping fund a campaign desire an ongoing relationship, especially communication, with the school system.

If the organizations contacted feel an honest effort has been made to communicate with them, and feel the direction of the school district has been clearly stated, they may not only become financially involved but may also become dedicated and committed to active participation.

Small, select groups, such as pastors and priests, carry great influence, as do medical professionals (physicians and dentists) and organized groups (other than the chamber of commerce) of industrialists or influential business people.

In the most successful campaigns that the authors experienced, each of these groups was used in a timely and beneficial way. Since there was a pastor on the campaign steering committee, he enlisted the active and positive support of the clergy in the community. The type of support this group can offer is varied and of great importance. The opportunity to address the members of local congregations through church bulletins, newsletters, and even through sermons delivered from the pulpit must be given great priority in any meaningful campaign.

Additional support and influence for a successful campaign comes from medical and dental professionals. People are used to soliciting and accepting the recommendations of these professionals, so where it is possible (and it is always possible to attempt to do so), support from the doctors and dentists of a community must be given high priority. In at least one such instance, the authors received voluntary participation from medical professionals who raised sufficient funds themselves to pay for several major ads and even signed the foot of the ad, urging support for the school issue.

Also in the mainstream of a community's leadership structure are industrialist organizations, manufacturer's associations, and so forth, whose impact can be quite significant even if their number is relatively small. When endorsements take the collective form of a large ad in the newspaper, including signatures of individual presidents, CEOs, or other officials, above their printed names and firm names (see Figure 1), voters are greatly impressed. In addition, such people may be effectively used as authors (or signers) of letters sent to the editorial section of a newspaper. Where willingness exists and where the individual industrialist is held in sufficient esteem and respect by employees, it is useful to send a letter to employees over the signature of the firms' president, CEO, or other official (see Figure 2).

Figure 1

A MESSAGE TO ALL REGISTERED VOTERS IN THE PIQUA SCHOOL DISTRICT:

Dear Voter:

We, the undersigned Piqua Area Manufacturers wish to go on record as supporting the high school bond issue.

We realize the value of a quality education for our children and our employee's children. We want that education to be the very best in order to develop our children as future community leaders for Piqua.

Property taxes paid by Piqua industry provides over half of the total needed to build and operate our school system. Our taxes will increase. We feel that this increase is necessary to improve the resources which we all draw upon and benefit from.

We solicit your support for the bond issue and we hope that the new high school will be a source of pride and value for Piqua for many years to come.

C.R. Alexander
President
Crayex Corporation

Daniel P. French
Executive Vice President
The French Oil Mill Machinery Company

Rex McClure
President
Miami Industries

Earl F. Sever
President
Piqua Steel Company

Darrell F. Barbee
President
Piqua Poultry Company

Jerry Grooms
Branch Manager
Buckeye Bearing & Transmission Co.

Louis L. Mikolajewski
Secretary-Treasurer
Piqua Emery Cutter & Foundry, Inc.

Dick Siedel
Vice Chairman
Piqua Manufacturers Association

Kenneth J. Brown
General Manager
Professional Vehicle Division
(Miller Meteor)
Wayne Corporation

Ray Hammer
President
Hammer Graphics, Inc.

Dimitri Nicholas
Chairman of the Board
The Orr Felt Company

Richard A. Smith
President
Medalist Allen-A

Donald J. Byrnes
President
Quester Juvenile Furniture Co.

G.W. Hartzell
President
Hartzell Industries Inc.

Terry C. Pilon
Resident Manager
Container Corporation of America

Clifford J. Stein
President
Miami Metal Finishers, Inc.

Lewis E. Creager
Vice President
Piqua Pizza Supply, Inc.

Scott J. Hinsch
President
The Champion Cutter & Fixture Co.

Vincent Pisciotta
Executive Vice President & Gen. Manager
Perfecto, Inc.

Wilbur Sussman
President
Sussman, Inc.

William B. Decker
President
Val Decker Packing Company

Sam Jackson Jr.
President
Jackson Tube Service Inc.

Darrell S. Pothamus
Secretary-Treasurer
Quality Forms

Paul K. Thorn
General Manager
Forest Products, Inc.

Ross Donovan
Manager
Armco-Piqua Minerals

James F. Kerg
President
The Piqua Paper Box Co.

Ted Ristoff
General Manager
Bremco, A Division of [illegible] Inc.

Figure 2

CABLE ADDRESS: FRENCH PIQUA
TELEX NO. 288-009

FRENCH

PHONE—513-773-3420

THE FRENCH OIL MILL MACHINERY CO. PIQUA, OHIO 45356

Dear Fellow Employee and Voter:-

On Tuesday, November 7, voters in the Piqua School District (to whom this letter is addressed) have an opportunity to participate in a decision which will have a very important impact on our community, our company, and each of us personally.

For the past several years I voted for the High School Bond Issue somewhat reluctantly, because I still had several questions about the school. This year, I have finally realized that it is more important to focus on the important reasons for the new school, rather than to concentrate on the one or two detail-type questions which probably cannot be answered to every voter's satisfaction.

We all want our company to be successful, because as French Oil prospers, so do each of us, our families and our community. We need to have the best people we possibly can at all levels of our company. We have tried to recruit some sharp people, who decided not to come here to work, largely because of our schools—this hurts our company. Others have joined our French Oil team, but have not come to Piqua to live—this hurts our community, and reduces the number of available people to share the local tax burden.

We all want good medical care for our families. With the limited number of doctors in Piqua, Jean Burner often has to call on personal friendships to get medical care for our people. From my role here at the company, as well as my service as a Trustee of the Piqua Memorial Hospital, I know that we have made many efforts to recruit new doctors for Piqua. Although they liked our hospital, they questioned our present and future school facilities. Several candidates have gone to other communities as a result.

Piqua has not grown very much over the last several years. Growth may bring problems, but it also brings opportunities, which give our children a reason to stay here rather than seek their fame and fortune elsewhere. In the last 2 years, 6 firms have looked at Piqua as a place to locate and have gone elsewhere; the school facilities and non-accreditation was a factor in their decision.

Compare the high morale and achievements of the JVS graduates against Piqua Central graduates. A good school environment makes learning easier, helps the kids feel more positive about education, their community, and wanting to raise their own families here.

The French Oil Mill Machinery Company and the other Piqua business and industry will pay 58% of the cost of the new school, yet we strongly support it. Our company cannot vote for the school, but you and I can. This is the year. We have an opportunity to reverse trends which hurt our community, our company and our people. While our property taxes will go up a little, the increase will be minimized by the 40-acres of donated land for the high school and by the fact that an old bond issue is expiring. We can build the school before inflation raises the price. We can create a three school educational complex to really be proud of. We can make an important commitment to Piqua's future.

I feel that the big advantages far outweigh the disadvantages, and wanted to express my thoughts to you because the issue has a direct influence on our company, and thus on each of us. I urge you to vote FOR the High School Bond Issue, but however you feel about this, or the other issues and political races, please exercise the rights for which many Americans have fought and died. VOTE ON NOVEMBER 7.

Sincerely,

Dom French

D. P. French

Anticipating Problems and Hurdles Before They Occur

Although it is impossible to anticipate all of the problems that might become a part of a campaign, it is important that, if possible, some heavy, productive thinking take place. The letters to the editor columns of local newspapers are potential midcampaign disaster areas. Typically, these columns print, without comment, letters that are identified and signed from the newspaper's circulation area. It is a marvelous forum for the expression of positive and negative sentiments, generalities, half-truths, and the expression of false ''facts,'' figures, and assertions. Efforts to answer such misstatements, misrepresentations, or false information with follow-up letters from school supporters is too late to be of significant value. Too often, the resulting damage is done at the time the letter hits print, and there is very little that can be done about it.

When possible, it is of immense value to gain the commitment of the editorial staff (generally the editor) of area newspapers to provide an editor's note to statements that are outright false, that use wrong figures, or that present issues in an obviously untrue fashion. It is impossible to overstate the importance of this contribution. If a misstatement of fact or figure is followed by an editor's note providing the correct facts or figures, the potential damage done is corrected immediately. In addition to the apparent benefit, people who might involve themselves in a vituperative antischool campaign become aware that misstatements of fact will be corrected instantly by the editor of the newspaper, and there is less likelihood that such deliberate distortions of the truth will be submitted to the newspaper. Although many journalists are reluctant to commit themselves to the correction of error in a letter to the editor section, it is important that campaign leadership not shy away from making the request.

Chapter VI

Conducting the Campaign

Launching the Campaign

In any campaign, a formal launching should be established, accompanied by as much media attention as possible. There are at least two major points when the campaign commands news treatment from the media, as opposed to paid advertising. These include the opening of campaign headquarters and the formal kickoff of the actual campaign.

A campaign headquarters (if such a physical facility is available) can become a media event in itself. A ribbon may be cut signifying the opening of the campaign headquarters—and perhaps of the campaign itself. Appropriate signs indicating the identity of the campaign headquarters may be unveiled and presented by any sponsoring or underwriting organization to the campaign leadership. Campaign leadership may be introduced in conjunction with the opening of a campaign headquarters, and issues of particular importance to the campaign may be identified and addressed by them at that time. If there is donated space for campaign headquarters—that is, in a facility designated by a business firm, chamber of commerce, or other such organization—there is opportunity for promotional recognition of both the sponsor/benefactor whose facilities are being used, as well as the identification of that location as the hub of future campaign activities.

It is important that all area media (newspapers, radio stations, television stations, and any other area media) be advised of the opening of campaign headquarters. This is usually accomplished through a press release provided to the media several days in advance, with the request that it be carried as local news. It is useful to follow up on the press releases with either a personal or telephone call to the appropriate person in each of the local media. It is desirable that local media cover this campaign headquarters opening--a picture on the front page of the newspaper, a story quoting campaign leadership, a news story on local radio or television stations, and so forth, will provide an immense promotional boost.

Most campaigns begin with a kick-off. This may take the form of a luncheon or banquet provided to campaign workers and may include the steering committee and related leadership positions in the campaign, or if possible, all of the volunteer workers in the campaign organization. Although the inclination to do so is noble, in many cases it is not practical to provide a free meal to these individuals, since it may negatively impact the voting public. Thus, some form of meal provided by the individual workers themselves (a pot luck or buy-your-own) is more appropriate.

The most important contribution of a kick-off luncheon or banquet is its role as a media event. Again, it is critical that members of the local media be invited and encouraged to attend. It is impossible to overstress the importance of media involvement in such a kick-off banquet or luncheon. It is at such an event that the campaign's major issues can be identified and addressed in the most favorable of all settings. Wherever possible, a guest speaker or outside personality may be included in the kick-off luncheon or banquet to lend greater external credibility than individual members of the campaign organization can give. For example, a state legislator or other politician may be asked to summarize the current situations of the economy, the fiscal or tax structures, the legislative mood, projections, and so forth. It is important to determine the attitude and predispositons of politicians before including them on the program, however, to ensure their support of public schools.

If a market analysis was undertaken prior to the development of the campaign, it may be possible to coordinate the speaker with some of the issues it identified. For example, in one of the author's involvements in public school financing issues, prior market analysis determined that the major campaign issues were economic. Therefore, the speaker provided for the kick-off banquet was an economist from a regional university. This speaker was able to address the economic impact (see Figure 3) schools have on an individual community—on the school's role in attracting industry, jobs, residents, and so forth, into a community or encouraging those who are already there to remain. In that particular situation, the economist serving such a role—actually an econometrician—was able to develop an oversimplified econometric model of the impact of schools on a local economy and to present it to the campaign leadership and many of the volunteers at that time.

It may be reasoned that people who most need to hear such a message (those who need to be convinced of the need to support the operating levy or bond issue) are not in attendance at such kick-off programs. However, the ability to reach these people through the media will adequately substitute here. The speaker should be interviewed by radio, newspaper, and where available, local or area television stations. With a cooperative media, it is possible to reach thousands of voters without directly expending any precious campaign dollars.

Follow-Up of Known Positive Voters

Earlier sections of this publication have dealt with the identification of positive voters, both registered and unregistered—those most likely to support the issue.

From such precampaign and midcampaign efforts, a master list should be compiled of all positive voters, including those who are newly registered. It is essential that the compilation be centrally controlled, that it be broken down by basic voting areas (wards or townships and then by precinct and individual voting locations), and then alphabetized within each area and the address and telephone number of each person noted. The vital nature of this list should be clearly understood by all precinct and neighborhood campaign workers and its maximum use made in at least two ways during the final days and hours of the campaign:

1. Within the last two days prior to election day, all people on the master list of positive voters should receive a telephone call from their neighborhood, area, or precinct campaign worker urging them to vote and reemphasizing one or more campaign issue(s) and the great significance of their one vote.
2. On election day, there are requirements in many areas that a list of people eligible to vote be posted outside the voting area of each precinct (or voting location) and that, at one or more specified times during the day, the names of those who had already voted be checked off, lined out, or similarly eliminated.

Figure 3

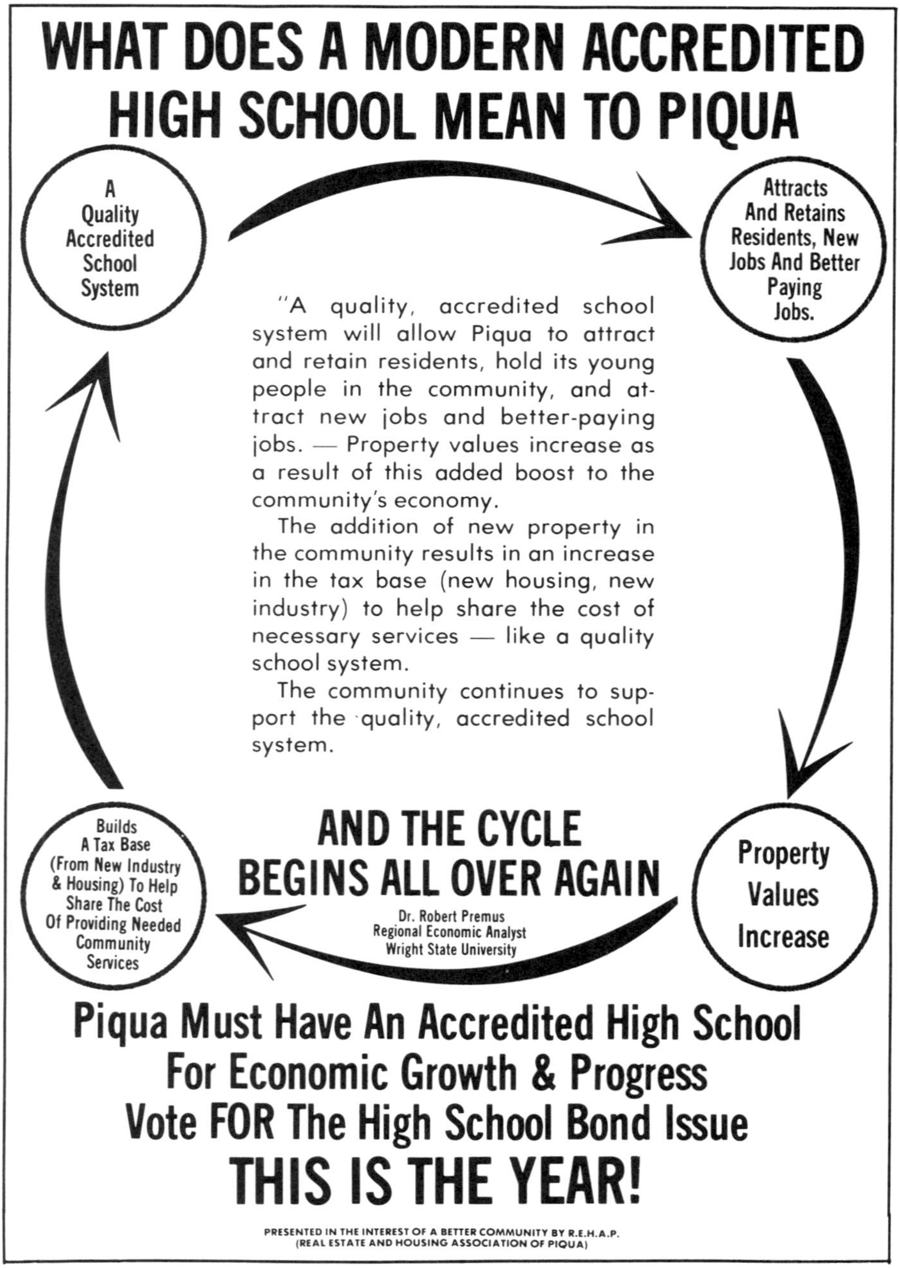
WHAT DOES A MODERN ACCREDITED HIGH SCHOOL MEAN TO PIQUA
A Quality Accredited School System
Attracts And Retains Residents, New Jobs And Better Paying Jobs.
"A quality, accredited school system will allow Piqua to attract and retain residents, hold its young people in the community, and attract new jobs and better-paying jobs. — Property values increase as a result of this added boost to the community's economy.
The addition of new property in the community results in an increase in the tax base (new housing, new industry) to help share the cost of necessary services — like a quality school system.
The community continues to support the quality, accredited school system.
Property Values Increase
AND THE CYCLE BEGINS ALL OVER AGAIN
Dr. Robert Premus
Regional Economic Analyst
Wright State University
Builds A Tax Base (From New Industry & Housing) To Help Share The Cost Of Providing Needed Community Services
Piqua Must Have An Accredited High School
For Economic Growth & Progress
Vote FOR The High School Bond Issue
THIS IS THE YEAR!
PRESENTED IN THE INTEREST OF A BETTER COMMUNITY BY R.E.H.A.P.
(REAL ESTATE AND HOUSING ASSOCIATION OF PIQUA)

This requirement is literally worth its weight in gold to the eleventh-hour effort in a campaign. It is worth diligent investigation into the existence of such a requirement and worth considerable effort to ensure its practice on election day.

Campaign workers, armed with an alphabetized list of known positive voters eligible to vote at their assigned polling place, must be at the polls shortly after each posting of the list. By simply checking off the names of the positive voters on their list who have already voted, it is possible to identify those who must be contacted prior to the time the polls close. By making such a comparison when the last posting occurs (generally 4 pm), campaign workers are able to make one last effort (pleading, if necessary) at getting positive voters to the polls. If, in these last-minute phone calls, you can offer to provide babysitting or transportation, you have a better chance of success. It is the authors' experience that it is possible to add a substantial number of positive votes in this way. It does require careful organization and additional hours of volunteer effort, but the payoff can be well worth any effort.

Converting Negative Voters

It is effective to impress volunteer workers with the impact that a change in one vote represents. All volunteers should realize that each time they contact and convert a person opposed to the levy or bond issue to a positive voter, they have effected a change in two votes--by subtracting one vote from the negative column and adding one vote to the positive column.

Use of People Who Are Visible in the Community for Individual Endorsement and Testimonial

In any community there are people who, because of their position or areas of responsibility, are more visible than the average citizen. These individuals often command positions of great esteem and respect. They include pastors, priests, doctors, dentists, business and industrial leaders. In other sections of this document it was indicated that, as members of a group (a manufacturer's association, a medical or dental society, a ministerial association, and so forth) these individuals can provide meaningful assistance both in the form of financial assistance to help underwrite the cost of campaign expenses and in the form of support and testimony.

In most situations, the testimonials should be a part of the media advertising program. A pastor, priest, dentist, doctor, or business or industrial leader may be used in a newspaper advertisement with a picture and a message urging the support of the issue for specific and identified reasons. It is important to realize the unique role that a campaign leader or promotional adviser has with such visible people in the community. Although a pastor, priest, or professional person may be accustomed to writing and speaking, it has been the authors' experience that these people are frequently willing to have an endorsement ghostwritten for them by someone with basic communication skills and a grasp of the campaign issues. It is strongly recommended that the people most involved with preparing promotional materials or directing the campaign itself be prepared to volunteer their services in writing endorsements. It is useful in discussing the matter with a pastor, doctor, industrialist, etc., to volunteer a sample outline of such an endorsement or script. Volunteers would then be invited to build their own communication style and personality into the script.

Thus, the campaign person is volunteering to develop the script or endorsement for community-visible people, to present it for the acceptance/modification/rejection of the visible people, and then to aid and assist in any modifications that are necessary. From the authors' experience, the visible people are very willing to have such assistance and most probably will accept, without significant modification, any script or copy that is prepared. This provides an enormous opportunity to the campaign leaders. They, in essence, speak through the mouths of people in the community who command respect and attention in addressing the issues campaign leaders wish to have addressed.

Figure 4 is an example of a draft letter to "Christian Friends" provided on two separate occasions to members of the clergy in a local community. The results of using that draft were outstanding. In several instances, sermons were drawn very closely from the draft letter. This use was not confined to Protestant pastors, but was used extensively in Catholic churches (a group thought by some not to be extremely supportive of public school financing issues). There are those who believe that clerics should refrain from any form of political activity, but as the social awareness of members of the ministry increases, it is possible to gain and use the active, aggressive support of these influential members of the community.

Figure 4

This letter was supplied to members of the Piqua Ministerial Association as a model for possible use in either a church bulletin or newsletter. Several variations of this letter were used by members of the ministerial association during the campaign.

(AN OPEN LETTER TO RESPONSIBLE, CONCERNED CHRISTIAN CITIZENS)

Dear Christian Friends,

The responsibilities and duties of a Christian are indeed many and varied. Our Lord left us with the "Great Commission" to go, and teach, and spread the good news of his coming (Matthew 28:19-20). A Christian's responsibility in carrying out that commission is quite clear. It is our most important work for His kingdom here on earth.

However, Christians are also called on to take the lead in caring for the needs of others in their family and in their community—in short to be a compassionate and caring part of this community. In this way we show God's love to those around us.

Although I realize that it is likely that some of you may not completely share my feelings in this matter, I must point out that in the upcoming November 7 vote on a bond issue for a new high school for Piqua I see an issue where we as Christians must take a stand for what is morally and economically right in our community.

Over the past eight years, citizens of Piqua have been asked repeatedly to support a bond issue to build a new high school. Each of the efforts has failed—sometimes by a very narrow margin. We will have another opportunity to vote on this issue on November 7. I feel that it is very much in the nature of Christian duty to take decisions very seriously, to consider the complete picture, and to commit the decision to prayer and to a searching for God's will for us and for our community.

I firmly believe it is my Christian responsibility to my congregation and to my community to support this bond issue, and to urge that you, too, support it with your vote on November 7. I have investigated the matter very carefully, and I feel this way for the following reasons:

1) Piqua badly needs a new high school facility! The present building is simply inadequate. The school has lost its North Central accreditation as a result, and this loss reflects badly on our community. Indeed to persons in other communities and to the world in general, it makes Piqua look like a city which simply *doesn't care* about its young people or their education.

2) Piqua needs to be able to attract additional jobs and better jobs to the community. Our young people too often must move out of the community in order to find adequate jobs. And when we lose our young people to other communities, Piqua—and the churches of Piqua—loses much of its most vital resources for the future.

As long as Piqua has a non-accredited high school, new jobs are not going to come into the community. Employers are simply not going to bring their people into a community with a substandard and non-accredited high school.

Even now our community is losing good people. I have seen the results of a study that shows that over 70% of salaried employees hired by Piqua firms in the past three years didn't move into Piqua—they chose other communities, and Piqua is the loser when this happens. And the most frequent reason given by such people is the "condition of the high school".

We have already lost many opportunities to attract new jobs to Piqua. According to a recent Piqua Area Chamber of Commerce study, at least *six* new industries investigated Piqua as a possible site for expansion during the past two years. They all spotted our inadequate, non-accredited high school, and NONE OF THEM CAME TO PIQUA with their jobs and with the tax revenue which additional industry brings!

Piqua has far fewer jobs per 1,000 population than any of the major towns of our size nearby (Sidney, Greenville, Troy).

All of these factors have a bad effect on Piqua's economy. They hurt property values, hurt our ability to retain our young people, and require that we pay a greater share of taxes for necessary public services (like schools) than we should have to pay.

3) The cost of a new high school is much less than many of us believe. I was very surprised when I checked and found just how small my increase in taxes would be—and I urge you to check for yourself. The information is available in the brochure which is being distributed throughout our community.

4) The cost is even lower now since the land for building the high school (40 acres) has been donated by the Garbry and Hartzell families—BUT ONLY IF A BOND ISSUE PASSES! The cost is still lower right now because we will soon have some of our newer elementary buildings paid for.

5) But the cost of a new school will keep getting higher. If we had built the school eight years ago when it was first proposed, it would have cost only about half of what it now costs, and if we should wait for eight more years, the cost will be over $18 million. How could we possibly afford that?

6) It won't cost anything to do the added bussing which will be required. Piqua will get an ADDITIONAL subsidy from the state (thus getting more of Piqua's tax dollars back from Columbus for use here in Piqua!) which will cover all the costs of adding busses, drivers, etc.

7) It is important to this congregation that our city have a modern and accredited high school. We need this for its impact on more and better jobs for ourselves and for our children and grandchildren; we need it for its impact on growth in our community, and for growth in our church (parish, etc.). (FOR THE CATHOLIC PARISH: we need it in order that our parochial schools might grow and prosper as more jobs attract more Catholic parents who will buy homes in the community, support our churches, and our parochial schools).

Please give these reasons your careful and prayerful attention. They went a long ways in convincing me.

It *is* hard to vote higher taxes on ourselves. It *is* tempting to say "NO" and save a little bit of our money. But the time comes when Christians must look beyond their past disagreements or judgments and stand up and be counted for what's right!

I believe that time is NOW. Let me earnestly encourage you to vote for the high school bond issue on Tuesday, November 7. It is not only vital for Piqua, its kids and its future, it's vital for US, and I feel it is very much a part of our Christian duty.

Sincerely,

(FOR MAILING OR BULLETIN INSERT PREFACED BY AN ACCOUNCEMENT FROM THE PULPIT OF WHAT IT IS AND URGING CAREFUL READING OF THE LETTER/INSERT)

____

Tax Table (A statement of the Price)

An essential ingredient in any marketing program is the establishment and use of a price structure to be presented to the market. It is no different in dealing with operating levies or bond issues. There is a price to be paid, typically in the form of an increase in property taxes. Voters tend to overestimate the actual price they may pay to support an operating levy or bond issue; the authors have found that they sometimes overestimate by a multiple of five to ten, which, of course, only serves to heighten the resistance of the voter.

There is considerable value in going to the market with a statement (as accurate and precise as possible) of the price associated with a levy or bond issue; therefore, the development of a table, which will present the price increase for each of many levels of property value, is an essential tool for any campaign.

There are a variety of ways a tax table can be presented. The most common attempts to relate the tax increase to the market value (or the assessed value) of property. In the authors' opinion, this is not the best comparison to use, due to the fluctuation in value of real estate. Except for people who have recently bought or sold a property, they have little grasp of their property's market value. Thus, any attempt to tie a tax increase to the market value of property would serve only to confuse the voter.

Most property owners tend to be more aware of the amount of property tax paid than of the current market value of property owned. For that reason, the authors have successfully used a tax table (see Figure 5) that compares the increase in property taxes with the present level of taxes paid. This table should include enough detail so people at a wide range of income levels will be able to determine their actual price increase.

Uses for such a table are numerous. Certainly a tax table should be included in any brochure developed for campaign use. In addition, the tax table may become a campaign tool for media advertising. Frequent presentation of the tax table in a newspaper advertisement is strongly recommended. In addition, the tax table can be combined with other appeals such as combining ads or flyers (presenting the price in the form of the tax table) with an appropriate concluding campaign message, such as "For such a reasonable price, how can we afford to say no to our schools?"

We also recommended that the tax increase be broken down into the cost per day. This results in the presentation of a relatively small figure when compared with other daily expenditures.

Accuracy is extremely important. It is vital that input be gained from a county auditor, treasurer, or equivalent authority. This means that a campaign leader must sit down with the official and figure the amount of tax increase represented by each point of the tax table. This may be more complicated than it first appears. In some states there are reductions, rollbacks, exemptions, and so forth, from a stated tax rate that will take effect before the actual increase can be determined. These factors are best addressed by the person dealing with them in preparing the individual tax bill—the auditor, treasurer, or other official. In addition, the amount of taxes collected for payments toward bond issuance typically vary during the life of the bond.

This variance usually translates into higher collection during the earlier years

Figure 5

WHAT WILL THE HIGH SCHOOL BOND ISSUE COST PROPERTY OWNERS OF THE PIQUA SCHOOL DISTRICT?

For The Average Family Owning A Home:
$14.64 Every 6 Months . . . 8¢ Per Day
For You???

If you paid this much in property tax (6 months) in July, 1978	The new high school will increase your half year taxes by approximately	And that increase per day would by only:
$ 25	$ 2.93	2¢
50	5.86	3¢
75	8.78	5¢
100	11.71	7¢
125 Average For Piqua	14.64 . . . Property Owner	8¢
150	17.57	10¢
175	20.49	11¢
200	23.42	13¢
225	26.35	15¢
250	29.28	16¢
275	32.20	18¢
300	35.13	20¢
325	38.06	21¢
350	40.99	23¢

* Average semi annual increase over the 21 year term of the bond issue; this amount includes the 4.94 mill bond issue, the .9 mill operating levy approved by the voters in 1973 and the reduction of 1.2 mills caused by retirement of earlier school bonds.

VOTE FOR THE PIQUA HIGH SCHOOL BOND ISSUE

- ✓ REGAIN ACCREDITATION
- ✓ RECEIVE 40 ACRES OF FREE LAND AS A BUILDING SITE
- ✓ BUILD NOW . . . AT TODAY'S PRICES EACH YEAR OF DELAY ADDS $1 MILLION TO THE PRICE

Presented In The Interest Of A Better Community By
Piqua's Active School Supporters, Beverly Pratt, Chm.

and lower collection during the latter years. When presented as tax table figures, however, they must be averaged and so indicated on the table. Accuracy maintains the credibility of the campaign organization. Temptations to present the average figures without explanation would open the door to future problems. Therefore, a footnote to the table should indicate that the figures presented represent an average increase in taxes paid over the number of years designating the bond's existence. This problem does not occur with an operating levy.

In most situations, it is possible for the county auditor or treasurer to identify an average tax bill for a residential property owner. Where this is the case, it is useful to pick out the average increase residential property owners in the district will be asked to accept. Once the identification of the average or typical increase on a per-day basis has been made, it is important to pinpoint the uses of this average daily cost increase. When the benefits and merits of support are presented in campaign materials, media advertising, and so forth, the daily average cost should be indicated. An advertisement highlighting the benefits and merits might close with the phrase "and all of this for just X cents per day."

There are some risks associated with the heavy use of such figures in campaigns. It is true that there is only one average property or individual in any area and that all other individuals or properties vary from that figure. Thus, it is impossible for all persons to associate or identify with the stated average figure. Presentation of a tax table showing the increased tax burden at many points, however, can overcome this difficulty.

In many areas, older people (generally aged sixty-five or older) living on limited incomes are given relief from property taxes in the form of a homestead exemption. The amount of such an exemption from payment of property taxes is often quite significant. As it may vary from 10 percent to 75 percent or more, the actual price to be paid could be substantially reduced. It is vital to determine the existance of a homestead exemption and, if available, to present it clearly and frequently to the market of older taxpayers, giving them a true picture of the total cost of their support. Failure to perform this step accurately may cost many votes on election day; performing this task effectively may add many positive votes.

Slide-Tape Show

In preparing for operating levy or bond issue campaigns, a slide-tape presentation, including background, appeals, and campaign should be considered. The guidelines for a slide-tape presentation are very basic:

1. Find people who are interested, capable, and have sufficient time to work on what could be the most effective "campaigner" of all.
2. Begin well in advance. Obtain and prepare the slides and develop the accompanying narrative at least six months before the election.
3. Present and emphasize factors that earlier market analysis determined may gain a favorable vote.

Technical assistance is usually necessary and, for this reason, it may be necessary to look to the school system's media director or to someone in the community with media interest. There may be a person on the staff of an area university or community college who specializes in media and could provide technical assistance.

Write a script with at least a basic outline of the points to be made and share it with people close to the scene to see that all important points are covered. It is crucial that the points from the market analysis be emphasized.

After the script has been tentatively set, it is time to obtain appropriate slides. Slides should be selected well in advance of the actual campaign, but space should be left in case it becomes necessary to add slides addressing late-developing key issues.

An accompanying tape that will automatically advance the slides is a great help if the people showing the slide-tape to the community do not have technical backgrounds.

Once the slide-tape show has been developed, it should be shown first to campaign workers so a full understanding can be gained, all questions answered, and any technical errors corrected.

When the slide-tape show has been formally approved by the campaign committee, appropriate community groups should be made aware of its availability through news media publicity. If a list is available, a special note can be sent from the campaign committee to each organization, indicating that the slide-tape show is available. It is also important to make religious groups aware of it, as many have services and fellowship hours where a showing of the slide-tape presentation can be effective. The slide-tape show can be the key to the entire campaign. If done properly, it is one of the finest ways of selling the program because it gives the community a consistent approach and can virtually serve as the speakers' bureau for the campaign committee.

Song

Development of an appropriate song can involve the student body in a positive manner. For the Piqua bond issue campaign, local teachers composed lyrics for the popular song, "Top of the World," sung by the Carpenters. Permission to use the music and put the following words to the music was obtained from the publisher:

> Such a feelin's comin' over us
> We are wonderin' just what is all the fuss-
> They have said you don't care
> And we don't think they're fair
> And we won't be surprised if it's not true.
> Everytime we meet the world head on,
> You've been helping us—it's good to know you're there.

And the pride deep inside
Makes us want to confide
That the nicest folks are Piquads, and they care
Get out and vote for the levy,
It's a vote for the future
And the only vote that counts is yours alone.
And the faith that you place
In the future human race
That faith puts YOU at the top of the world.

The song was sung by the school choir and used as background for advertisements on the radio. This used students in a positive manner, gave the advertisements some polish, and let the community know that students were part of the campaign.

Additional opportunities to sing may occur if there are choir concerts or if students are asked to present programs during community activities.

Question of the Day

Approach newspapers and radio stations well before the campaign to determine whether or not they would, without cost, publish or announce a question and answer provided by the campaign committee each day of the campaign. Set up a schedule so that the same question being used on the radio is also being used in the newspaper. The "Question of the Day" (see Figure 6) could be included in the newspaper in a corner of the front page, in a box, and could be scheduled at the radio station at the discretion of the station manager (preferably at the conclusion of each newscast). The schedule should be structured so that critical questions could be repeated several times during the campaign.

Figure 6

School Question of the Day

How much of the cost of building our new high school is to be paid by homeowners? Don't business and industry have to pay their share in this area?

They certainly do. More than half of the cost (58 percent) of our new school will be paid by the property taxes of Piqua business and industry. Homeowners will pay only 42 percent of the cost.

"I've Changed My Mind"

One of the best ways to influence people to support an operating levy is to use publicly the names of people who have been negative in the past but realize now how important the school issue is to the community. Carefully identify those who in fact have been negative. Some are very hesitant to publicly say that they have changed their minds, but in many instances those people who have been negative are not ashamed to admit it. Having a script already prepared can sway many who are reluctant. This concept can be used in newspaper advertising by including pictures of the people, their addresses, and the reasons they have changed their minds. For radio, people are asked to go to the radio station and prepare a tape (scripted with assistance, if needed), identify themselves (including address), and indicate why they have changed their minds.

This can be a significant way of changing minds on an issue. Many willing to do this are average citizens, others well known. Either is valuable. It is easy to identify with people who have changed their minds and have enough courage to say "I changed my mind, and I now support the school issue."

Brochure

A brochure is also crucial to a campaign. A brochure must be completed very early in the campaign and should be developed by people who are close to the scene and are aware of pertinent ideas and issues. Work on a brochure should begin at least three or four months before the actual election date so it can be completed and ready for distribution at least two weeks before the election. The brochure should be printed in black and white to avoid angering citizens who assume the brochure is financed by taxpayers.

The brochure is a bit like the slide-tape presentation—it must emphasize campaign issues. The document should spell out the accomplishments of the school district and specifics that everyone should be proud of. The brochure should be easily read and contain relevant pictures. Where an "up-front" market analysis has been done, the issues revealed should be addressed and developed in the brochure. A tax table and most of the "Questions of the Day" should be included in the brochure. It should be brief enough for perusal in five to seven minutes. See Figure 9 for an example of the front and back covers of a successful brochure.

Cable TV and Radio Call-In Programs

Use community cable television and radio stations to advantage by planning a call-in program. A call-in program is very helpful, since it gives the campaign committee a chance to answer questions that emphasize the major campaign issues. It is also a good way to determine and answer questions that are prevalent in the community. It is wise to have several people and telephones at the site to take the questions. Reserve the right to screen out questions that are totally inappropriate for the occasion.

It is important to have a panel that is representative of the entire campaign, including board of education members, campaign chairs, and school administrators. It may even be appropriate to include students, teachers, ministers, and others who add a different perspective to the questions or to the campaign itself. Introduce and close the program with the campaign song, if available. If a slide-tape presentation is being used in the campaign, it should be used at some point in the television call-in. The call-in program must be properly publicized so the community is aware of it. In smaller cities, it may be held at a school rather than a studio.

One bit of effective strategy is to have members of the campaign committee prepared to call in. In this way, important questions and concerns are certain to be addressed, and answers can be prepared in advance. Both the radio and the CATV call-in programs are best toward the end of the campaign when specific issues or questions need to be clarified, addressed, or refuted.

Figure 7

"I've Changed My Mind. . ."

"For the past eight years, I've voted against each of the high school bond issues in Piqua. On November 7th, I'll be voting FOR the new high school, and so will my wife, Helen. We've changed our minds, and here's why: We have FREE LAND to build the new school on . . . 40 acres of it . . . and we've never had that opportunity before. We also like the location of the new school. It makes sense to put the high school in the same general area as the JVS and our community college. And when we learned that building and operating the new school would add just 8¢ a day to our taxes, it became clear that this is a bargain that we shouldn't pass up again.

When you think about it, as we did, I'm sure you'll see that it makes sense to vote FOR the high school bond issue on Nov. 7."

Charles E. Morris, Sr.
520 Second St.
Piqua, Ohio

IT'S TIME TO TAKE A STAND

PRESENTED IN THE INTEREST OF THE COMMUNITY BY
PIQUA'S ACTIVE SCHOOL SUPPORTERS, BEVERLY PRATT, CHAIRMAN, 512 CALDWELL

Figure 8

"I'VE CHANGED MY MIND"

Rev. Edward B. Fischer
1615 Washington Ave.
Piqua, Ohio

"My wife, Evelyn, and I have lived and served in the Piquarea for 40 years. I love Piqua, but I've never voted for a high school bond issue — I've never been convinced that Piqua really needed it — until this year! On November 7th, both Evelyn and I will be voting FOR the high school bond issue. Let me tell you why. I feel that our community badly needs to get accreditation back for the high school. I know that industry is passing Piqua by, and our community loses jobs when this happens. I know that many good people working in Piqua have chosen to live in other towns — because of the high school. And I know that the only way to change all of this is to regain accreditation for our high school — and the only practical way to do that is to pass the bond issue on November 7th and build that new school. It scares me to think of how much more expensive it will be if we wait — and with FREE LAND to build on now, we've got to get the job done. Please join me. I've changed my mind, and after you take a close look at the facts, I hope you do too."

Vote "FOR"
The Piqua High School Bond Issue
IT'S TIME TO TAKE A STAND

PRESENTED IN THE INTEREST OF A BETTER COMMUNITY BYPIQUA'S ACTIVE SCHOOL SUPPORTERS, BEVERLY PRATT, CHAIRMAN, 512 CALDWELL

Figure 9

THIS IS THE YEAR . . .

Pictured above is a mass model of the proposed Piqua High School. It does not show specific building details such as doors, windows or the type of brick exterior.

Note: Figure 9 is continued on page 56.

A Note From P.A.S.S.

Dear Friends,

We have presented in this booklet information which we honestly believe completely supports the urgent need for a new high school building in Piqua.

We are asking you now to put aside any negative thoughts you may have and to look directly at the needs of our young people and the city of Piqua. We implore you to consider how many tax dollars we have wasted by delaying so long, and how much more costly the building will be if we continue to delay.

November 7 is a very critical day for the citizens of the Piqua School District. We have an opportunity on that day to open new doors for the youth of Piqua. By doing this we are encouraging the progress and development of the Piqua area, and attracting more and better jobs for Piquads present and future. Please join with us as we pass this bond issue to build — on donated land — the new and modern building which will allow us to regain North Central Accreditation for Piqua's high school.

Thanks in advance for your support.

PIQUA'S ACTIVE SCHOOL SUPPORTERS (P.A.S.S.)

Beverly Pratt, Chairman

A "YES" Vote Means:

Regaining accreditation for Piqua High School.

Receiving FREE LAND for the high school site.

Attracting new and better jobs to Piqua so that our young people will remain after they graduate.

Saving taxpayers' money by building at today's prices.

Holding our tax increase to a minimum — under 5 mills.

Adding to the value of our property by making our community a more attractive place to live.

Attracting new residents to buy homes and spend their dollars in Piqua.

Relieving overcrowding at the junior high schools.

Providing the best in quality education for our youth.

A "NO" Vote Means:

Continuing loss of accreditation - Piqua being the only non-accredited high school in the Miami Central Conference.

Losing free land — the land will be donated only if a bond issue passes.

Continuing to lose new and better jobs along with many of our finest young people as they can find jobs only in other communities.

Wasting more money as we watch construction costs increase by over $1 million for each year we delay.

Increasing our taxes even more in the future.

Continuing to lose new residents and their tax dollars.

Overcrowding at the junior high schools.

Providing inferior facilities for the education of our youth.

PHS

YES X

This is the year!

Paid for by Piqua's Active School Supporters (P.A.S.S.). 400 N. Wayne St., Piqua, Ohio. Beverly J. Pratt, Chairman

Media

The success of any issue is dependent on a healthy, open, and honest relationship with the news media.

The Newspaper

The newspaper's treatment of school issues is extremely important. Consider the following avenues:

1. *General coverage.*
School district news is usually covered on a regular basis by a newspaper reporter. It is important that a good relationship be established with not only the reporter but also the publisher and editor. During any school year, the news media should receive current information about positive activities occuring in the school district.

2. *Letters to the editor.*
During the course of the campaign, there may be reason to have citizens write letters to the editor on behalf of the cause. This is designed to promote key points in the campaign. Approaching publishers of the newspapers to ask if they would share, in advance, negative letters with the committee is suggested. If a letter is misleading, the committee would have an opportunity to respond or add an editorial comment. Frequently, people whose names or positions are visible in the community are willing to have letters written for them. Given the opportunity, the campaign committee should stand ready to draft such letters and the volunteering author given ample chance to revise or rewrite the letter before it is sent to the newspaper. An alert campaign organization can often gain valuable support and influence through the media by exploring this opportunity aggressively.

3. *Editorial endorsement.*
It is always helpful to get editorial endorsement of the newspaper for the school campaign. This can be cultivated well ahead of time by developing a good relationship between the school and the newspaper personnel.

4. *School page.*
In many communities, a section of the newspaper is regularly devoted to school news. This area should be explored by school officials and campaign people as a campaign is underway. This is an excellent way to promote issue benefits for students and to have the youngsters express their opinion about the necessity of the issue.

5. *Question of the day.*
Earlier, the "Question of the Day" was addressed. This can be very helpful in promoting the very crucial aspects of the campaign.

6. *Paid advertising.*
Do not underestimate the importance of paid newspaper advertising. Many post-election reports show the influence of paid advertising, especially in the newspaper, to be significant. It is also important for businesses that advertise to include a positive "slug" in their ads near election time; for example, "Vote yes for our school's future."

7. *Some Possible Advertising Ideas for the Newspaper:*
   a. *I changed my mind.* Discussed previously.
   b. *Ministerial endorsement/advertisement.* Discussed previously.
   c. *Staff endorsements.* Another advertisement (with much lower priority) could include the names of staff members of the various school buildings in the district.
   d. *Parochial endorsement.* An ad including the names of parent-teachers or staff of one of the nonpublic schools supporting the issue is beneficial.
   e. *Doctor/dentist endorsement/advertisement.* Discussed previously.
   f. *Manufacturers association endorsements/advertisements.* Discussed previously.
   g. *Personal endorsements.* The use and effect of personal endorsements, especially via paid advertising, may be questionable, but it is an avenue to explore. When used, each ad should address a specific campaign issue. The person making the endorsement should be carefully selected for relevance to that specific issue.
   h. *Economic appeals.* See Figure 10.

Radio

The support of the radio stations and their personnel is also important to the campaign. In addition to normal coverage of school activities, radio can be used with several approaches.

1. *Question of the day.*
The same approach used in the newspaper could be used on the radio.

2. If the superintendent has a weekly radio program, that time can be used to promote various aspects of the campaign without actually urging people to vote yes.

3. *Call-in programs.*
Discussed previously. This can be done via radio, television, or both.

4. *Editorial endorsement.*
In some communities, radio station management may be willing to publicly endorse the campaign and its purpose.

Television

1. *Call-in programs.*
Discussed previously.

2. *Weekly TV program.*
If the school district has cable television, it should have already contacted the CATV people about regular programs through which to promote school activities. Near the end of the campaign, be certain the time is spent to promote the issues developed from the earlier market analysis.

3. *Special programming.*
It will be helpful to prepare videotapes on specific aspects of the campaign. A program to introduce the campaign leadership might be effective. Another program

Figure 10

STOP PAYING

"INFLATION TAX"

For EACH YEAR we wait to build a new accredited high school, WE LOSE.

$1,000,000 TO INFLATION

IN BUILDING COST INCREASES!

That loss equals a cost of $40 per year for every man, woman, boy & girl in the Piqua School District—and for a typical family of four the annual inflation cost is $160.

LET'S MAKE THIS THE YEAR WE SAY GOODBYE TO "INFLATION TAX"

Vote "FOR" the Piqua High School Bond Issue

The Cost To The Average Piqua School District Family Owning Property is— **8¢ A DAY**

WE MUST BUILD NOW:

- REGAIN ACCREDITATION FOR OUR HIGH SCHOOL
- GAIN 40 ACRES OF FREE LAND—AS A BUILDING SITE
- STOP PAYING "INFLATION TAX"

IT'S TIME TO TAKE A STAND!

Presented in the interest of a Better Community By Piqua's Active School Supporters, Beverly Pratt, Chairman, 512 Caldwell

would discuss the real issues of the campaign and, in almost every campaign, one of those issues would be economics. In addition, a program that explains the benefits to older citizens through the Homestead Exemption Act could win many senior citizens' votes.

4. *Public service announcements.*
Many cable television operations have a channel referred to as a "weather screen." This channel gives pertinent aspects of the weather, but a portion of the screen includes other short messages for people viewing the channel and can be used to promote the campaign. In many cases, the cable television staff will consider this message a public service announcement and offer it at no cost to the campaign committee.

5. *Paid advertising.*
Be sure that enough time is spent in preparing copy, that copy is appropriate and consistent with the issues identified in any earlier market analysis, and that the tapes to be used are recorded by people who have effective speaking voices. Where possible, an appropriate song (addressed earlier) can be used as a lead-in, as an ending, or can be played softly under the entire advertisement. See Figure 11 for examples of radio advertising scripts.

Figure 11

Sample Radio Advertising Scripts

Script A

This is Kent Wise. I'm a sophomore at Piqua Central, and I'd like everyone to know that all of the kids in the class of 1981 are looking forward to being the first class to graduate from the new high school you'll be approving on November 7th. And I can promise you we'll be taking plenty good care of it. Actually, the many kids who have used the present building—including many of *you—have* taken good care of it. Sure Central is old; it has been used—by about a thousand kids a day for over 60 years—but it's not abused—we really do appreciate all that you've done for us—and thanks so much for voting FOR the high school bond issue. Believe me, we won't let you down. (Close with campaign song)

Script B

(With two voices);

#1: You folks in Piqua are really SLY.

#2: How's that?

#1: You're getting more of your tax dollars back from Columbus to use right in your own community.

#2: We are? How are we doing that?#1: When you build your new high school, you'll be bussing more students of course. All the kids in grades 9 through 12 will be eligible to be bussed. But the State pays a subsidy—an extra subsidy you don't get now—for each kid bussed. So, boy, do you gain. You're going to transport more students—and you get back more of your own money from Columbus to work for you right in Piqua. You win all the way around!! Sly!

#2: Yeah, maybe we're sly—but I think we're just plain smart—and we'll all play it smart when we vote FOR the Piqua high school bond issue on November 7th. This is the year.

Script C

This is ______________. My wife and I live in Candlewood on New Haven. I've never voted FOR a Piqua high school bond issue before, but on November 7th, I will be! Let me tell you why I've changed my mind. I've found out that the extra cost is a *lot less* than I had thought it might be. I also really like the fact that our high school students will be able to get free transportation from their neighborhoods to the new school. And that's great for kids from Candlewood and from East Piqua (Shawnee) where we operate our store. And the extra bussing ISN'T GOING TO COST US A DIME. The State will pay our school system for each extra student we transport—and that extra state money will completely cover all of the extra bussing costs. I think it's great that we'll be able to get more of our tax dollars back from Columbus to work for us here in Piqua. Sure, I've changed my mind! Please join me in voting FOR the high school bond issue.

Development and Use of Letters to Employees

In addition to the endorsement of business and industrial leaders, it is important that leaders be used in as many other ways as may be deemed effective.

One of the most important contributions that an employer/business/industrial leader can make to a campaign is a pronouncement, plea, or some other form of communication to employees. Figure 2 (page 37) provides a sample letter written with the authors' assistance. Although this letter may represent an extreme position and an enormous commitment on the part of its author, the general format is applicable to many situations. The opportunity to address such an issue and identify how the merits are likely to affect the local economy and the specific business involved is extremely important.

One significant warning must be attached to this recommendation—not all business and industrial leaders are popular with employees. In some situations, the friction resulting from labor-management relations and negotiations (and, in recent years, the cutbacks made in jobs) have undermined the respect and trust necessary for business or industrial leaders to be influential. Therefore, go slow with this type of campaign tool. Acknowledge and carefully evaluate, on a situation-by-situation basis, any potential for backlash. The potential for adding votes is great if the impact, credibility, and other assets of the letter's author can be assured.

Conducting Tours of Present Facilities

The authors have found that market research conducted prior to a campaign will identify that those who have recently been inside a school building or involved in its programs are most likely to be positive voters. As a result, it may be as important to introduce people to the school program and facilities as to reach them with any form of campaign literature or promotions. Recognizing this fact is easy; making it work to benefit a campaign is often much more difficult.

In some communities, PTA or PTO organizations can be effective in promoting prospective voter participation in tours, presentations of school programs, activities, and so forth. Expect low attendance at such programs, however. Experience leads the authors to believe that most people are willing to accept what they feel they know rather than risk being wrong.

Student involvement is vital here. They can conduct tours of present facilities, demonstrate the effectiveness of various programs, and, most importantly, reach people and encourage them to attend. Invitations from students can be delivered through the media (radio, TV, newspaper advertising), or printed and delivered to parents and neighbors. Demonstrating student commitment to the school's programs can be highly effective.

If campaign materials—brochures, tax tables, a slide-tape presentation, and so forth—are available during tours, they would be employed to the maximum. All slide-tape shows should be introduced and shown, a copy of the campaign brochure given to each individual attending, and additional copies provided to those interested in distributing them among their friends and neighbors. Since these tours can produce additional volunteers, it is an appropriate time to ask for additional help.

Windshield Project

Another way involving the students in a campaign is to ask community service station operators for permission to allow students to offer to wash the windshields of all customers on a particular Saturday morning. When the students do this, they conclude by giving the driver a card that says "We were pleased to clean your windshield. We hope you can see your way clear to vote YES on ________."

This is a gimmick, but it does serve several purposes. It gets the students involved, it gets the people who run the service stations committed, and it gives the motorists a chance to see the young people in the community doing something to promote education.

Bank Statement Stuffers

Nearly every financial institution sends customers a monthly statement. Enlist the cooperation of local institutions to include a stuffer in each statement. The stuffer, sized to fit into the envelope without folding, should emphasize an important aspect of the campaign.

Since statements are mailed on a rotating basis, arrangements must be made well in advance. The campaign committee provides the stuffer, and the financial institution will likely do the rest, as long as the stuffer does not add to their normal postage charge.

Menugram

If the school's lunch menu is distributed in newsletter-type fashion, it is possible to use the reverse side of the menugram to promote campaign issues. The menugram would be distributed to elementary students, who would take them home to parents.

Lapel Badges

As the campaign organization becomes known around the community, it is helpful to identify workers. Lapel badges—paper name tags that slip into clear protective covers—worn by campaign workers can be a positive influence in the community.

Athletic Events

Home football or soccer games may be used to promote a fall campaign for an operating levy. For a midwinter campaign, use basketball games and for spring, use baseball and softball. Information and inserts on the issue can be included in the program that is usually available. Members of the campaign committee can also pass information out as people walk into the ballgame.

Display a sign below the scoreboard promoting the issue. Public address announcements, prepared by the campaign committee and provided to the public address announcer, should be read throughout the game.

Public address announcements should be short, emphasizing the main points of the campaign. Even though some people are offended by hearing these announcements during games, they can be effective to promote a point. In most cases, positive people will be in the majority at these activities, but if this is a concern, the promotional information can be printed on stickers that can be placed on the front of a program.

Table Tents

It is a standard procedure in some campaigns to make table tents for placement in restaurants and school cafeterias to promote specific issues.

Town Hall Meetings

It is important to provide a forum where citizens in the community can express their views. A town hall or similar meeting should be organized to give the board of education members, school administrators, and campaign officials the opportunity to answer any questions the community might have. This is a good defensive measure to neutralize the *we-weren't-given-enough-facts* criticism. Citizens who come to town hall meetings most often ask questions that enable a reaffirmation of campaign points. If questions are based on erroneous information, the meeting provides the committee an opportunity to publicly correct the misinformation. This is especially helpful if the media attends (make certain they do) and reports on the issues discussed. In most cases, attendance is sparse, but it is important to listen to the community. As with the call-in programs, it is helpful to have ''plants'' ask questions that should be addressed.

Parade

If the time of the year is appropriate, consider holding a parade on the Saturday before the election. A parade can include many groups—the high school band, vocal groups, and student groups (including elementary youngsters) marching through the community with banners and information to pass out to people along the parade route.

The parade should go to the downtown portion of the community and assemble for brief remarks from citizens, board members, administrators, campaign chairs and others who can give extra emphasis or reasons people should vote for the levy or bond issue. A parade is a bit unique and can be effective.

Model of Building

Depending on the market analysis results, there may be some merit in having a scale model of any proposed building or addition. The model gives people a visual appreciation of the building and can be very effective if the survey uncovered a need for more specifics about the actual configuration, size, and so forth.

Have the architect prepare the model. In most cases, they can be convinced to do this without charge, since they won't get a contract if the issue doesn't pass.

Floor Plan

Results of a market analysis may show that a floor plan of any new building or addition is needed if a bond issue is being promoted. This is important to some people so they can visualize what they are actually supporting. Again, the architect is the person to contact about providing such a floor plan. School officials should be certain that the floor plan is consistent with specifications drawn up by the school district. It is very important that the floor plan be produced in a professional fashion and duplicated for distribution to the community at meetings, service club organizations, and at any time the bond issue is being discussed. It must provide sufficient detail, including number of rooms, size of rooms, activity areas, and gyms.

School Lunch Week

It may be wise to denote the week before the election as an ''education week'' for the community, and to draw attention to the election by doing something special for school lunches. Enlisting visible members of the community, such as business and industrial leaders, to serve food at the cafeteria on one of the days will likely attract media attention because it is unique. As students go through the lunch line on that particular day, a card is given to the youngster to take home. The card could say ''As a part of Education Week, it was our pleasure to help serve lunch to your child. We hope you will help us better serve our children and our community by voting YES for the operating levy [or bond issue].'' The impact can be even greater if each of those serving that day, in that particular building, signs each one of the cards. This is a good way to get visibility from industrial and community leaders and to show that they support the school's efforts. It is also a unique way of communicating with the parents.

Chapter VII

The Special Roles

The Board of Education

The role of the board of education is paramount in any campaign. The board of education is responsible by law for providing adequate funds for school operation and appropriate facilities for the boys and girls they serve. Because they have to make the decisions that result in bringing an issue before the people, the board of education becomes the focal point of a campaign.

The board of education should be doing considerable preliminary work based on information from the superintendent and staff regarding the needs of the school district. It is obvious, therefore, that the chief school administrator is responsible for keeping the board of education informed of the need to consider operating levies or bond issue campaigns. It must be recognized, of course, that the board of education as a body must eventually make the decision.

The board should make decisions early enough to meet the requirements of the law, and to ensure that a proper campaign can be planned. Early planning is essential to any issue. A lack of time to plan an issue diminishes its chances of approval by the voters and could even be construed as a lack of vision on the part of the board of education. Whenever possible, the vote of the board to place the issue on the ballot should be unanimous. Split votes present extra difficulties for a campaign.

The board of education should consider every campaign as one that belongs to the people. Their firm belief in that philosophy is the key to the passage of a levy or bond issue. After they have made their decision, the board should be prepared, with the advice of staff members, to appoint a campaign committee and to give that group much latitude in forming and implementing the campaign. The board of education can enhance the status and effectiveness of the campaign committee by announcing its public approval.

The campaign committee should be representative of the community. School personnel should be in minimal numbers and maintain a low profile. The committee should include a member of the board of education and be composed of people who are interested and supportive but who are willing to commit themselves to the many hours of work it takes to put the campaign together.

The board must place a great deal of confidence in the campaign committee. Trust the committee to act in the best interest of the school district and give them latitute to make decisions that promote the issue. The committee should never forget that many campaign decisions eventually become policy decisions that can only be made by the board of education.

The board members should and can be very active during the campaign, but they should not be too visible. When members of the board of education are too prominent, voters can consider it as an indication of insufficient interest or commitment on the part of the general community.

The board of education members can do many things during the campaign. They can serve as speakers, make television tapes, participate in town hall meetings and call-in programs, and they can be responsible for a message of support in the district newsletter.

It is essential that all campaign materials to be distributed to citizens be approved by the board of education. This ensures that a campaign committee does not make statements that would eventually conflict with policies the board of education cannot support.

The Superintendent of Schools

The initial responsibility of the chief school administrator is to accumulate all necessary information for the board of education. The board then considers both long-term and short-term ramifications and decides what is to be presented to the voters. The superintendent also outlines the issues to be decided by the board of education many months before their actual placement on the ballot. Early preliminary work is absolutely essential, as citizens may perceive last-minute proposals as weak or unplanned.

After the issue is officially placed on the ballot, the role of the superintendent may change to a large degree. In many campaigns, the superintendent of schools maintains a high profile and is considered to be the person who runs the campaign committee. Depending on the results of the market survey, the superintendent may wish to continue exerting leadership but maintain a low profile and work behind the scenes.

If the commitment to a campaign steering committee is total, and if the board of education has complete confidence in this group, the steering committee may occasionally make a decision that is contrary to beliefs of the superintendent. It is vital that the superintendent and the campaign committee mutually understand that the superintendent is a member of that committee, but one having no veto power. It is essential that the steering committee consider the superintendent's perspective and understand that the only time the superintendent will interfere with the decision-making process is if the steering committee is promoting something that violates a formal position taken by the board of education.

The Administrative Team

The administrative team members should be actively involved in compiling and inputting information for the superintendent to forward to the board of education. This ensures that their feelings and insights are included in the package presented to the voters.

The administrative team should be represented on the campaign committee, and provision should be made to release them from school duties to participate in the planning and implementation of the campaign.

It is imperative that all of the administrative team members (not just those on the campaign committee) are aware of the aspects of the campaign. Primary sources of information could include an administrative team newsletter that would deal almost exclusively with planning the campaign. The superintendent could also begin the administrative team meetings with an update on the campaign. By doing this, the administrators will be aware of the progress of the campaign and, in turn, will share the information with the rest of their staff members.

It is also important that administrative team members be active participants in the campaign and that they urge their staff members to do the same. There can be much evidence of a campaign in the buildings, but it should be subtle enough to be effective without intimidating or overwhelming those who visit the building. It may be helpful for administrative team members to share with the superintendent and the campaign committee their thoughts on how to promote the issue. This will prevent activities that appear to be effective in one building but are counterproductive to the total effort.

If the administrative team members have citizens' advisory councils, it may be appropriate to place the campaign on the agenda at one of the council meetings. Building principals can effectively bring people up to date on the campaign, without suggesting how they should vote, through their regular parent newsletters. Obvious political pleas can prevent the the use of a bulk rate mailing permit.

It is important to be sure that all of the buildings in the district have campaign materials on hand. In this way, administrators can answer questions or clarify issues from telephone callers or visitors. Administrators should funnel those questions they cannot answer to either the campaign committee or to the board of education office. Administrative team members could also wear lapel badges indicating their support of the issue and daily promoting the issue's necessity.

It is important that the administrative team members be formally and publicly thanked at the end of the campaign and, if there is a victory party, they should be invited.

The Certified and Classified Staff

The campaign committee should have a representative from the teachers' association and from the classified staff. Provision should be made to allow them time—off work, if necessary—to participate in program planning and implementation. It is important for them to be aware of what the campaign committee is doing so they, in turn, will feel a part of the total process and will share that information with co-workers and neighbors.

Certified and classified staff members can also show support in a campaign by wearing badges or buttons and by being well informed and able to answer questions from the community. It is important that the community not perceive them so aggressive that their support has a negative effect. Communities can be very sensitive to the use of school time to promote the issue.

Staff members should be very careful to avoid any type of threats to students about the ramifications of parental nonsupport. It is imperative that the campaign committee, superintendent, or administrator ensure the staff members understand their role in communicating with students during their regular class period. This avoids the accusation that staff members indoctrinate the students, who go home and try to pressure parents into supporting an issue.

Staff members should be thanked after the campaign, whether or not it was successful. It is important that they know their active participation was appreciated.

The Students

The use of students in an operating levy or bond issue campaign is controversial. There are those who feel the use of students is unwise because it invites accusations of exploiting youngsters who do not have to worry about paying higher taxes. Although this is sometimes an accurate assessment, there is also the feeling that the students can be involved in a campaign without being exploited.

The use of students requires a committed staff member to act as liason with a small group of interested student leaders. The enthusiasm of that staff member, whom the youngsters can rally around, in many cases adds to their enthusiasm and dictates the breadth of student activity.

A student should be included on the campaign committee. A mature young person can be released from school and can add a great deal to the planning and implementation of a campaign. A student feels honored to be a part of the committee and can involve other students.

The students can do many things to assist. They can write letters to the editor. If there is a student page in the local newspaper, they can write articles supporting the levy and point out specific aspects of the levy or bond issue that benefit students. It is appropriate for students to communicate to the community how the passage or loss of an issue will affect their education. In many cases, student pleas are more effective than the concerns of adults.

In addition to writing activities, there is word-of-mouth contact with their parents, neighbors, and friends. They could organize a student parade, pass out literature, wear sandwich boards around the community near the date of the operating levy or bond issue, or record the campaign song for use as an introduction to radio advertising. The use of students in preparing promotional television or radio tapes can be effective. (See Figures 12, 13, and 14 for examples promoting and demonstrating student involvement.)

The Architect

If a bond issue is being promoted, the architect can also play a role in the campaign. In some campaigns, many questions are asked about the building itself and can best be answered by the person who will design the construction project. In some instances, a scale model and a floor plan of the proposed building are helpful to community members who tend to be negative unless then can see what they are "buying." The architect can be of great assistance in this particular area.

Questions can become crucial in the eyes of some voters, so the architect's availability at public meetings can be psychologically advantageous for the campaign committee. For those architects who are reluctant to participate, the superintendent might offer this suggestion: "If you want the contract—participate."

Figure 12

Student Involvement Memo
(for Assembly Program—Pre-election)

What Secondary Students Can Do for the Levy

(Or How a Kid Can Vote—Several Times)

I. Understand the issues:
   - A. Get familiar with the fact sheet:
     1. "What happens if the levy passes?"
     2. "What happens if the levy fails?"
   - B. Know how the cuts will affect you—your brothers and sisters, your friends, etc.
   - C. No more high school—or JVS, or Lehman—bussing.
   - D. No bussing for junior high or elementary students who live within two miles of their school.
   - E. No more sports, band, drama, or clubs, after January 1st.

II. Hunt—really hunt—for people who you are sure will vote for the levy.
   - A. Who are they?
     1. Family members
     2. Neighbors
     3. Family friends
     4. People at church
     5. People where you work
   - B. How do I convince them to vote for the levy?
     1. You may not need to convince them, simply tell them how concerned you are that the levy passes and how its loss will affect you—your friends, your school, etc.—you may find that they quickly agree with you and indicate that they intend to vote for the levy too. If they don't indicate openly that they intend to support the levy, you can assume they probably aren't supporters—or that they are "on the fence" and their vote could go either way!! In that case, show them the "fact sheet", go over it with them, then leave the fact sheet with them, and try to talk to them later in the campaign.
   - C. What do I do with people who are convinced and indicate they will vote for the levy? How about people whom I can convince? That's the biggest role that you can play—you can:

III. Be sure that they vote on Tuesday, November 3
   - A. Remind them the weekend (or the day) before—or both. (This assumes you have recorded their name and address and phone number

so you can stay in contact with them after you've learned that they are a "yes" voter)

B. Contact them on Election Day—don't give up trying until you reach them and learn for sure that they have voted. Let them see how hard you're working and how much this levy means to you!
C. Take them to the polls if they need a ride—or:
D. Babysit for them while they go to vote.
E. BE SURE THEY VOTE!!
The polls are open until 7:30 P.M., so keep working with "your people" right up til that time!

Remember:

This is the way You Can Vote!!

(And if you contact several people, and get them to the polls to vote for the levy, you can really feel like you've voted many times!!)

Don't forget Mom and Dad!! Be sure they vote as early in the day as possible. Then perhaps they can help you contact those of "your people" and get them out.

Good Luck—and Thanks.

P.A.S.S.
Piqua's Active School Supporters

Figure 13

"We sure appreciate the great support you gave our M.C.C. Championship Basketball Team last season. You helped so much!! We also appreciate everything you provided for us during our school years—super teachers—fine programs—good facilities. We're proud of our hometown, and we hope we can always make you proud of us as graduates of Piqua Schools.

ANDY WARNER

RANDY GABRIEL

But OUR SCHOOLS NEED OUR HELP, and we need to ask you to join with us in helping KEEP Piqua schools great!

We really want to see the younger kids of Piqua have the same opportunities and the same programs we have had.

ONLY YOU CAN HELP US—AND HELP OUR PIQUA SCHOOLS

KENT WISE

RODD ZELLER

WE WILL BE VOTING FOR THE 5.5 MILL PIQUA SCHOOL OPERATING LEVY ON TUESDAY

PLEASE JOIN US!

VOTE FOR THE CONTINUED STRENGTH OF PIQUA SCHOOLS BY SUPPORTING THE OPERATING LEVY. THANKS FOR YOUR SUPPORT."

Andy Randy Kent Rodd Jeff Dave

IT'S UP TO US!

JEFF HILL

DAVE KASLER

Presented in the interest of a better community by Piqua's Active School Supporters (P.A.S.S.) Jack Neuenschwander, Chairman

Figure 14

AN OPEN LETTER TO OUR HOME COMMUNITY . . . FROM A FEW OF ITS RECENT 'PRODUCTS.'

November 3rd! What's so special about it? Just another Tuesday, isn't it? NOT AT ALL!!

TOMORROW—November 3rd, 1981—will be a "MAGIC DAY." On that day, citizens of Piqua will show "their" kids that THEY CARE ABOUT THEM! They know that if THEY don't care, no one else will.

We are just a few of the 272 who were the first class to graduate from the new Piqua High School last year. We can't say enough as to how proud that makes us. We speak for all P.H.S. students in saying "Thank You" to all who agreed that our town desperately needed that new school. We appreciate what was done for us, and some day we will do the same thing for our community's young people.

Another desperate situation has arisen, and we're confident it will be solved tomorrow. It involves the 5.5 mill operating levy that is so vital to education in Piqua—as we know it!

How vital is it? We can't even imagine what it would be like without extracurricular activities in our schools.

Just to think about it:

No football games to look forward to—

A closet full of bright, new band uniforms not worn all fall—

A brand new—but silent—gymnasium in the heart of winter—

A sports page of excelling area athletes and teams, minus any Piqua representatives—a Wednesday paper without any "Smoke Signals"—

The absence of clubs and organizations—

Christmas Season without any Christmas Vespers—

Spring without a school musical—

All those buses sitting idle—

So many teachers—gone—not replaced—and class sizes so much larger—grim—

Students with nothing to do, but get into trouble—

Just to name of few—

All of these possibilities are a terrible thing to read about, much less to experience.

Fortunately these things will not have to happen because of the "MAGIC DAY" that comes tomorrow.

And that is where YOU come in!

We have sent our (absentee) ballots home, or we'll be home to vote. We're confident that YOU WILL HELP so that Piquads can once again show their kids they DO CARE about them.

We want to be a part of giving our young people what WE received—a well-rounded education!

Tomorrow is truly a "SPECIAL DAY" in the lives of each Piquad, young and old. Just as our motto reads "Piqua, City of Opportunity," let's make sure all Piqua kids have that opportunity. TOGETHER WE CAN! Together we can make this happen by passing the school operating levy.

BRING ON OUR "MAGIC DAY!"

You're great, Piqua, we love you!

Sincerely,

GARY WILES—BOWLING GREEN
KIM MCMAKEN—OHIO NORTHERN
LARRY WILES—UNIVERSITY OF TOLEDO
ANGIE TYLER—OHIO NORTHERN
RANDY GABRIEL—SOUTHWEST LOUISIANA
NICKI ADAMS—EDISON STATE
DAN MCMILLAN—OHIO NORTHERN
MARTY ARY—OHIO UNIVERSITY
RODD ZELLER—OHIO WESLEYAN UNIVERSITY
KENT WISE—TAYLOR UNIVERSITY
DONNA APPLE—MIAMI UNIVERSITY
CARL BLEMAN—EDISON STATE
JEFF HILL—UNIVERSITY OF TOLEDO
JIM JENNINGS—UNIVERSITY OF TOLEDO
BETSY BERTLING—EDISON STATE
DAVE KASLER—
BARB BUTSCH—
DAVE MELLOR—UNIVERSITY OF TOLEDO
TERRI CHRONERBERRY—WRIGHT STATE
BRIAN HILDEBRAND—OHIO NORTHERN
JAMES VALANDINGHAM—MANCHESTER
KEVIN BACHMAN—HEIDELBERG
MELISSA FEFREE—UNIVERSITY OF CINCINNATI
GREG HARRIS—TAYLOR UNIVERSITY
ANNE GILMORE—OHIO NORTHERN
PHIL PUTERBAUGH—EDISON STATE
TONI HARDENBROOK—EDISON ST
CURT SOUTH—OHIO STATE
TRACY HONEYCUTT—BOWLING GREEN
TOM STACY—OHIO STATE
LISA KAZER—MIAMI UNIVERSITY
GREG WHEELER—TAYLOR UNIVERSITY
CHRISTINE MENGOS—MIAMI UNIVERSITY
TIM WINANS—MIAMI UNIVERSITY
ANN SIEGEL—MIAMI UNIVERSITY
RHONDA SORRELL—MIAMI UNIVERSITY
LYNN STUMP—SAUDER FASHION SCHOOL
LYNN VON ASCHEN—BOWLING GREEN
ANDY WARNER—WRIGHT STATE

Presented in the interest of a better community by Piqua's Active School Supporters (P.A.S.S.) Jack Neuenschwander, chairman.

Chapter VIII

Post-election Analysis of the Effectiveness of Campaign Strategy and Tactics

In any well-organized and carefully implemented campaign, there will be at least one strategy employed and several tactics used. It is useful to learn which of the strategies and tactics were the most (and least) visible, which were well received and which were not, which were deemed as effective in causing positive votes and which were not.

To measure such reactions, some form of post-election study must be made. The study can be done by mail (with a random selection of registered voters sent a questionnaire), telephone, or personal interview. The relative strengths and weaknesses of each technique were discussed earlier when a pre-election study was recommended.

A basic structure of such a study should likely include the following:

1. An enumeration of the visible tactics, promotions, ad hoc events, advertising themes, and personalities used, with the request that respondents indicate which one(s) they had seen during the campaign.
2. A request that respondents indicate (by number) which five of the members of that enumerated listing were the most influential in communicating to or in convincing them to support the issue. Figure 15 presents the results from the authors' Piqua campaign.
3. A request that respondents indicate, from the five chosen above, which they felt to be the single most effective in communicating with, and convincing them (see Figure 16).
4. Questions concerning the age, sex, area of residence, and other demographics should be asked of respondents. In addition, a question should attempt to identify how the respondent actually voted (in favor or against) the issue. Each of these variables can be useful in analyzing responses to the visibility and effectiveness of the various campaign elements. It is important to know which campaign elements were more successful with women, men, older people, those who claim they supported the issue, and so forth. Don't be surprised if a post-election attempt to categorize respondents as voting for versus against the issue reveals that an overwhelming proportion claims they voted yes. This is a typical finding, and it will lessen the validity of the portion of a post-election analysis seeking to determine which campaign factors worked best among those who voted yes. This weakness should not eliminate the use of post-election analysis effort.

Figure 15

Top 15 Promotions and Activities in Ability to Make Registered Voters' Five Most Important List

Promotion Activity	Proportion Selecting It as One of Five Most Important or Useful
1. Newspaper ads	46.9%
2. Brochure	38.8%
3. Question of the Day—newspaper	35.2%
4. "I've changed my mind" ad—newspaper	29.2%
5. Radio Ads	26.5%
6. Tax table (approximate amount of increase in taxes) from regular newspaper ads	25.2%
7. Scale model	23.2%
8. Slide-tape presentation	15.2%
9. Question of the Day—radio	13.6%
10. Radio ad featuring students	10.4%
11. Pastor or priest urged members of congregation to support	9.6%
12. Live cable-TV call-in	9.2%
13. Personal visit from friends or neighbor	8.8%
14. Personal tour of high school building	7.6%
15. "I've changed my mind" ad—radio	7.2%
16. Speaker at a club or organization	7.2%

Figure 16

Top 10 Promotions and Activities in Ability to Make Registered Voters' Single Most Important List

Promotion Activity	Proportion Selecting It as the Single Most Important
1. Newspaper ads	10.8%
2. Tax Table (approximate amount of increase in taxes) from regular newspaper ads	10.1%
3. Slide-tape presentation	9.2%
4. Brochure	9.2%
5. "I've changed my mind" ad—newspaper	6.9%
6. Personal tour of high school building	5.6%
7. Question of the Day—newspaper	4.0%
8. Pastor or priest urged members of congregation to support	2.8%
9. "I've changed my mind" ad—radio	2.7%
10. Radio ad featuring students	2.1%

Those successful techniques and strategies for which there is research support in the literature are listed, with references, in Appendix C.

A Concluding Caveat

We have presented a case study, enriched by additional experiences, of the successful adaption of marketing tools to the campaign for public school operating levies and bond issues.

It is our hope that you are now armed with a set of ideas, many of them new. Please don't hesitate to innovate. Creativity and originality are nearly always a virtue in addressing the problems confronting the administrators and supporters of our communities' schools.

Some of the preceding strategies, tactics, and ideas will succeed for you—others may not. Some require considerable manpower and financial support to be effective. Some can be implemented with minimum personnel or budget support.

We would encourage you to let us know how well our prescription items apply—or do not apply—as you use them in your communities.

Good luck in your efforts to apply such marketing strategies and tactics in your future campaigns.

Appendices

Appendix A

Good morning, I'm ______________. I'm working with a research team. I'd like to ask you some questions about the way you feel concerning Piqua City Schools. I'm not even going to take down your name. I'm only interested in your answer, not in who you are. Will you be kind enough to chat with me on this subject for a while?

I'd like to read you a series of statements. Please tell me for each of them whether you

1 Strongly agree with the statement.
2 Agree with the statement.
3 Are uncertain about the statement.
4 Disagree with the statement.
5 Strongly disagree with the statement.

_____ 1. In general, Piqua has an effective school system.
_____ 2. A modern high school building in Piqua would make it easier for Piqua to attract new industry and new jobs to the city.
_____ 3. I believe what the school board says when it tells me of needs for our school system.
_____ 4. Students at Piqua Central are destructive and inconsiderate of school property.
_____ 5. High school teachers in Piqua do a good job of educating our children.
_____ 6. The facilities at Piqua Central are as good as those in neighboring communities.

Following are a number of possible uses to which the present Piqua Central building could be put if a new high school is built. Please indicate, if you can, which of them would be your FIRST, SECOND, and THIRD choices. (NOTE TO INTERVIEWER: GIVE SHEET "B" TO INTERVIEWEE. PLACE A 1 BEFORE THE RESPONDENT'S FIRST CHOICE, A 2 BEFORE THE SECOND CHOICE, ETC.)

_____ 7. A center for senior citizen activities.
_____ 8. A storage facility to be used by the Board of Education.
_____ 9. A center for adult education.
_____10. An elementary school.
_____11. A junior high school.
_____12. Administrative offices for the Piqua City Schools.
_____13. Offices for other government agencies.
_____14. Headquarters for the Red Cross, United Fund, etc.
_____15. Use the high school auditorium for public events (plays, concerts, etc.)
_____16. Make no use of it—tear it down.
_____17. I really don't have any preference for uses for the present building.
_____18. Other suggested uses—please specify.

____

_____19. If Piqua had built a new high school five years ago, which of the following do you think would have been the approximate total cost at that time?

1. $1 to $2 million	5. $8 to $10 million
2. $2 to $4 million	6. $10 to $12 million
3. $4 to $6 million	7. $12 to $15 million
4. $6 to $8 million	8. Over $15 million

_____20. If Piqua built the same new high school today, which of the following do you think would be the approximate total cost? (SAME CHOICES AS IN #19.)

_____21. If Piqua should build that same new high school five years from now, which of the following do you think would be the approximate total cost? (SAME CHOICES AS IN #19.)

_____22. If you could choose the design of a new high school, would you make it:

1. All on one floor.
2. Two floors.
3. It would make no difference.

_____23. If you could choose the location for construction of a new Piqua high school, which of the following alternative sites would you prefer?

1. A site east of Piqua, relatively near the Piqua East Mall, the JVS, and Edison State College.
2. A site east of Piqua, but not near the Mall, the JVS, and Edison State College.
3. A site on the west edge of Piqua.
4. A site southwest of Piqua in the area near the Candlewood Hills subdivision and Eisenhower park.
5. I have no strong preference as to a site for a new high school.
6. Other preferred site—please specify.

____

_____24. If a high school building site was selected which was different from one you prefer, what would your reaction be?

1. You would have no reaction. You would still vote for a new high school.
2. You might vote against a new high school because such a site was chosen.
3. You would definitely vote against a new high school because such a site was chosen.
4. You would vote against a new high school regardless of the site.

(NOTE TO INTERVIEWER: DO NOT READ #5 TO RESPONDENT. SIMPLY RECORD A 5 IF RESPONDENT REFUSED TO ANSWER. DO NOT PUSH FOR AN ANSWER HERE.)

5. Refused to answer OR no response.

_____25. If a high school bond issue were presented without any specific site included, how would you react?

1. You would surely vote against it if no site were specified.
2. You would likely vote against it if no site were specified.
3. You doubt if it would make any difference in the way you would vote.
4. It certainly would not affect the way you would vote.

_____26. If a new high school site had to be appropriated from its present owner (taken by the school board with the present owner paid a fair price for the land), how would you react?

1. This would not affect your willingness to vote for a new high school.
2. This might cause you to vote against the new high school.
3. This surely would cause you to vote against the new high school.
4. This would not affect you, but it would directly cause people you know to vote against the new high school.

Persons who have been opposed to increasing taxes to build a new high school have done so for a variety of reasons. For each of the following, please indicate how important it would be in causing you to hesitate to vote for a new high school.

1. Very important. It would likely keep me from voting for a new high school.
2. Somewhat important. It might keep me from voting for a new high school.
3. Not important. It would not keep me from voting for a new high school.

_____27. I don't want to see property taxes increased. (Would that be very important in making you hesitate to vote for a new high school; somewhat important in making you hesitate to vote; or not important to you in voting for a new high school.)

_____28. The present Piqua Central building would not be adequately used if a new high school building is built.

_____29. Since we have the Upper Valley Joint Vocational School (JVS) we don't need to pay for another high school.

_____30. The present Piqua Central building is good enough to serve as a high school as it is.

_____31. Students are disrespectful of property and would soon damage and vandalize a new building.

_____32. The present Piqua Central building could be repaired and renovated and remain in service for many more years.

_____33. School buildings should be financed through taxes other than property taxes.

_____34. The site selected—50 acres last time—was and is too large and costly.

_____35. Discipline among students in high school is not strong enough.

_____36. I don't want to help pay for a new high school which has carpeting in it.

_____37. A site was selected different from one which I preferred.

_____38. I don't want to help pay for a new high school which would be air conditioned.

_____39. It would cost too much to operate a new high school building.

_____40. Teachers in the school system are not effective.

_____41. The Board of Education hasn't always been truthful with the citizens of the school district.

_____42. I resent students from my neighborhood having to be a part of the Piqua School District.

_____43. The schools today teach too many "frills" and not enough of the basics (the 3 R's, etc.)

_____44. Teachers are too aggressive and militant in their demands for salaries, working conditions, etc.

_____45. Other factors—please specify:

____

____

(NOTE TO INTERVIEWER: SHOW INTERVIEWEE THE RESPONSES THEY PICKED AS IMPORTANT.)

_____46. Which of the factors above do you feel is the SINGLE MOST IMPORTANT to people who are opposed to building a new high school in Piqua?

_____47. Which do you feel is the SECOND MOST IMPORTANT to people who are opposed to building a new high school in Piqua?

_____48. Is Piqua Central High School presently accredited by the regional accrediting association (North Central)?

1. Yes 2. No 3. Not certain

(NOTE TO INTERVIEWER: IF RESPONDENT ANSWERS "NO", ASK:)

_____49. What do you understand to be the main reason that Piqua Central is not accredited?

(NOTE TO INTERVIEWER: <u>DO NOT READ THE CHOICES TO RESPONDENTS.</u> SIMPLY CLASSIFY THE RESPONSE AS IT IS GIVEN, AND RECORD ITS NUMBER.)

1. Inadequate physical facilities (high school building).
2. Poor teachers.
3. Poor programs (curriculum).
4. Any response related to student-discipline, etc.
5. Other—please specify _______________________
6. Unable to answer.

(NOTE TO INTERVIEWER: IF RESPONDENT ANSWERS "YES" OR "UNCERTAIN" TO QUESTION #48 OR IF RESPONDENT INCORRECTLY IDENTIFIES THE REASON FOR ACCREDITATION LOSS IN QUESTION #49, EXPLAIN TO THEM THAT THE HIGH SCHOOL LOST ACCREDITATION THIS PAST YEAR DUE TO INADEQUATE PHYSICAL FACILITIES AT THE HIGH SCHOOL.)

_____50. Among high schools in Ohio which are approximately the same size as Piqua Central, what percent do you believe are accredited by the North Central Association?

1. Fewer than 20%
2. 21% to 50%
3. 51% to 70%
4. 71% to 90%
5. More than 90%
6. No answer

Indicate for each of the following statements about the loss of North Central accreditation whether you:

1. agree with the statement.
2. disagree with the statement, or
3. are uncertain about the statement.

_____51. Having Piqua Central accredited by North Central is important to the Piqua City Schools.
_____52. Having Piqua Central accredited by North Central is important to the students who graduate from the high school.
_____53. Having Piqua Central accredited by North Central is important to the City of Piqua.
_____54. Having Piqua Central accredited by North Central is important to you.
_____55. Piqua should immediately build a new high school in order to regain North Central accreditation.
_____56. I am very disappointed that Piqua no longer has an accredited high school while such cities as Troy, Covington, and Sidney do have accredited high schools.

Following are some factors which might be important in encouraging you to vote for an increase in taxes to build a new high school. Please indicate for each of them whether it is:

1. Very important. It would encourage me to vote for a new high school.
2. Somewhat important. It might encourage me to vote for a new high school.
3. Not important. It would not encourage me to vote for a new high school.

_____57. Having a high school at least as attractive as towns like Troy, Covington, and Sidney.
_____58. Being able to regain accreditation from North Central if it built a new high school.

_____59. Enabling the high school and Bennet and Wilder Jr. Highs to have a "closed" lunch hour thus reducing some of the problems around these schools.

_____60. Seeing the young people of junior high and high school age actively campaigning for a new high school.

_____61. Building now will cost less than if we wait until a later time to build a new high school.

_____62. Gaining additional industry and jobs by having a more modern high school.

_____63. Educating students better in a modern, well-equipped high school building.

_____64. Having my property value decreased if Piqua does not have a new high school building.

_____65. Being prouder to live in the Piqua school district if we had a new high school.

_____66. Having a site selected and available for inspection well ahead of the voting day.

_____67. Having the proposed new high school enthusiastically endorsed by the business and industrial leaders of Piqua.

_____68. Having taxes increased less if we build now rather than at some time in the future.

_____69. Giving students at Piqua Central facilities as good as students at the Joint Vocational School.

_____70. Having a new four-year high school to eliminate overcrowding at the junior high schools.

_____71. Having a complete diagram and floor plan of the proposed new building printed and distributed well in advance of voting day.

_____72. Having a scale model of the proposed new building available for careful public inspection.

_____73. Having a layout of the proposed high school staked out on the site so that you could walk through it.

Other factors—please specify any other factors which might cause you to be encouraged to vote for a new high school.

____

____

(NOTE TO INTERVIEWER: SHOW INTERVIEWEE THE RESPONSES THEY PICKED AS IMPORTANT.)

_____74. Of all the factors mentioned above, which one would be the SINGLE MOST IMPORTANT to YOU in encouraging you to vote for a new high school?

_____75. Which factor would be the SECOND MOST IMPORTANT to YOU in encouraging you to vote for a new high school?

_____76. Have you been inside Piqua Central high school within the past three years?

1. Yes 2. No 3. Not certain 4. No response

So that the answers that people give us to our questions can be analyzed properly, I'd like to ask you a few questions about yourself. Remember that you are one of the several hundred persons being interviewed, and you will not be identified in any way with the way you have answered our questions.

_____77. Are you currently registered to vote?

1. Yes 2. No 3. Not certain 4. No response

NOTE TO INTERVIEWER: DO NOT ASK THE SEX AND RACE DEMOGRAPHIC QUESTIONS. GET THEM FROM OBSERVATION.

_____78. Sex: 1 Male 2 Female
_____79. Race: 1 White 2 Non-white
_____80. Age: 1 29 or younger.
2 30 to 44
3 45 to 59
4 60 or above

_____81. Have you ever had children enrolled in the Piqua public schools?

1. Yes 2 No

_____82. Do you presently have any children enrolled in the Piqua public schools?

1. Yes 2. No

(FOR THOSE WHO ANSWER "YES" TO #82):

Which school(s) do your child/children presently attend? (CHECK AS MANY AS APPLY)

_____83. Favorite Hill
_____84. High Street
_____85. Nicklin Ave.
_____86. North Street
_____87. South Street
_____88. Springcreek Twp.
_____89. Staunton St.
_____90. Washington Twp.
_____91. Bennett Jr. High
_____92. Wilder Jr. High
_____93. Piqua Central High School
_____94. Upper Valley Joint Vocational School

_____95. Do you have children in any of the parochial schools?

1. Yes 2. No

(FOR THOSE WHO ANSWER "YES" TO #95):

Which parochial school(s) do/does your child/children presently attend? (CHECK AS MANY AS APPLY)

_____St. Mary's
_____St. Boniface
_____Lehman High School
_____Other

_____96. Where do you normally do most of your grocery shopping?

1. Grissoms 3. Fulmer 6. Ulbrich 8. Don't know
2. Kroger 4. Marsh 7. Other 9. No answer

_____97. What is your religious preference? (What is your religion?)

1. Protestant 3. Jewish 5. None
2. Catholic 4. Other 6. No answer

_____98. Do you _______ the home presently live in?

1. Own 2. Rent

_____99. To the best of your memory, did you vote the last time a bond issue for a new high school was on the ballot? (This was presented at the June, 1976 primary election.)

1. Yes 3. Not certain
2. No 4. Refused to answer

(FOR THOSE WHO ANSWER "YES" TO #99):

_____100. To the best of your memory (and it would be very helpful if you can recall) did you vote for or against the last (June 1976) bond issue for a new high school?

1. For 3. Not certain
2. Against 4. Refused to answer

(FOR THOSE WHO ANSWERED EITHER "FOR" OR "AGAINST" IN QUESTION #100):

To the best of your memory, what SINGLE THING MOST CAUSED YOU TO VOTE AS YOU DID ON THE LAST BOND ISSUE FOR A NEW HIGH SCHOOL?

FOR: ____

AGAINST: ____

_____101. If there was an election held TODAY, and you were asked to consider a bond issue to be used for construction of a new high school, how would you be most likely to vote?

1. For 3. Not certain
2. Against 4. Refused to answer

(NOTE TO INTERVIEWER: SOME PERSONS MAY ATTEMPT TO AVOID ANSWERING THIS QUESTIONS WITH RESPONSES LIKE "IT'S MY BUSINESS," "I DON'T WANT TO TELL YOU," ETC. WHEN YOU RECEIVE SUCH A RESPONSE, EXPLAIN TO THE RESPONDENT THAT "MOST LIKELY WHEN A PERSON WON'T INDICATE WHETHER THEY WILL OR WILL NOT VOTE FOR SUCH AN ISSUE, IT REALLY MEANS THAT THEY WILL VOTE AGAINST THE ISSUE: IS THAT WHAT YOU'RE TRYING TO TELL ME? Don't press too hard, but try to get an answer—avoid using this follow-up approach on persons who genuinely seem uncertain.)

(ASKED ONLY TO THOSE WHO INDICATE A CHANGE FROM THE JUNE 1976 VOTE:)

Your answer indicates that you would likely change from the way you voted on the last high school bond issue. Can you tell me what causes you to make this change?

CHANGED IN FAVOR:

CHANGED AGAINST:

(ASKED ONLY TO THOSE WHO
1. ARE PROPERTY OWNERS, AND
2. WHO INDICATED IN QUESTION #101 THAT THEY WOULD VOTE FOR A BOND ISSUE TODAY)

_____102. Miami County property has been reappraised recently, and when you receive your next tax bill in late January 1978, you will likely find that your property taxes are somewhat higher. Suppose that in January you find that your property taxes are 15%-20% higher as a result of the reappraisal. Would this have any effect on how you would vote on new high school?

1. No effect. I'd still certainly vote for it.
2. Unlikely, I'd probably still vote for it.
3. Likely to cause me to vote against a new high school.
4. Certain to cause me to vote against a new high school.

_____103. Finally, if you had a choice between the following alternatives, which one would you consider to be the most realistic?

1. Use the present high school building without any remodeling or renovation.
2. Spend approximately $3 million to remodel the present high school building. This would not include any physical education facilities or structural changes to the building.
3. Spend approximately $6 million to renovate the present high school building, including an addition to provide facilities for physical education. Such a plan would require relocating students for about two (2) years while structural changes are done to the building.
4. Spend approximately $7 million to build a new high school, which would include physical education facilities.

_____104. Which of the alternatives above (and choose as many as you feel apply) do you feel would enable Piqua to regain accreditation from North Central?

1. #4 only
2. #3 and #4 only
3. #2, #3, and #4 only
4. All four of them
5. None of them
6. No answer

THANK YOU VERY MUCH FOR YOUR
ASSISTANCE AND COOPERATION.

Evaluation by Interviewer

At the conclusion of each interview (and before continuing to another interview) write your evaluation of the respondent and the interview in terms of sincerity and honesty of answers, any "between the lines" comment or reaction you felt from the respondent, and the extent of commitment to present position of the respondent.

Then evaluate the respondent as:

_____105. 1. Firmly committed FOR the new high school.
2. Tending to be FOR the new high school.
3. Totally uncommitted.
4. Tending to be AGAINST.
5. Firmly committed AGAINST.

For any respondent who appears to be either "Firmly For" or "Tending For," please note the address so that further contact may be made if:

1. Respondent is UNREGISTERED _______ (please check)
2. Respondent seems potentially willing and capable to assist in any upcoming campaign _______ (please check)

Address: ____

Appendix B

Volunteer Script for Location of Positive Voters

"Hi! I'm one of your neighbors. I live . . ."—(if on the same street or nearby, point to your house, otherwise give the name of your street and/or sections of town)."

(Note: The reason for having the volunteers do this is to clearly indicate to the person that they are part of the community, not someone who has been let out of a van only to be picked up later.)

"I've been asked by the Campaign Committee to distribute some literature later on—would you be interested in receiving some?"

(If the person says "No", thank them and say...) "If you change your mind, please don't hesitate to contact me."

(Leave—do not do any campaigning at this time.)

(If the person says "Yes", say...)

"Since I don't want to give you more than you need, what topics concern you the most?"

(or)

"I'll probably be getting a good bit of literature, what do you consider to be the major issues of the campaign?"

(If the person mentions negative things, such as "I don't want my taxes to go up", or "Teachers' salaries are too high," or "We don't need more bussing," etc., say...)

"Well I hope the information I give you will clarify these for you. I'll be seeing you just as soon as I obtain the literature."

(Leave—do not do any campaigning at this time.)

(If the person mentions positive things, such as "I don't see how teachers survive on such low salaries," or "We've got to do something to improve the education for our children," "I'd sure like to see what the new building will look like," etc., say...)

"I'm sure I'll have just the information you need. I'll bring it by just as soon as I get it. (Pause) Say, are you registered?"

(If the person says "yes", say...)

"That's great! Be sure and vote (give date.) We need your support."

(Take down their name and address.)

(If the person says "No, I'm not registered," give them the registration material and say...)

"Here is all you need to get registered. I'll be glad to help you." (Take down their name and address.)

Appendix C

The following table includes those successful campaign techniques and strategies for which there is research support in the literature. Much of the literature offers suggestions and opinions, but no supporting evidence. The references cited in this table refer to studies where evidence of a positive effect was obtained. Numbers listed at the end of each item correspond with like-numbered references under the "References for Table 1" section.

Table 1
Successful Campaign Techniques and Strategies

A. Use of crosspressure, i.e., giving voters information that will encourage the positive voters while giving the negative voters pressure that keeps them home. For example, mentioning the positive beneficial things schools do, or detailing the detrimental effects of a no vote. 6, 10
B. Slide-tape show. 5, 11
C. Person-to-person campaign. 5, 7
D. Use of print-brochures, newsletters, newspaper advertisements, etc. 2, 4, 5, 10
E. Solid facts that are difficult to rebut. 2, 4, 10
F. Market survey. 3, 5
G. Involve the architects, (build models, develop plans, provide funds for hiring consultants). 9
H. Tax table. 2
I. Support of city council, business, and industrial community. 2, 4
J. Providing transportation to the polls. 1, 4
K. Identification and follow-up of yes voters. 1, 6, 8, 9

References for Table 1

1. Bainbridge, William L., *An Analysis of the Relationship Between Selected Economic, Social, Demographic and Election Variables and Voter Behavior in Ohio School District Property Tax Elections*. Doctoral dissertation, The Ohio State University, 1979.
2. Fischer, Guerin A.,"Winning is the Name of the Game," *Community and Junior College Journal*, November 1978.
3. Harrison, Charles H., "In bond campaign, publicize the need, not the proposal," *Nation's Schools*, March 1972.
4. Keith, Pat M. and Rita Braito, "School Reference Directions for New Research," *Education and Urban Society*, VII, November 1974.
5. Konick, Emery Jr., "A miracle—on you can," *The American School Board Journal*, October 1978.
6. Lutz, Frank W.,"For Referendum Success! Convince your friends and confound your foes before they vote," *The American School Board Journal*, February 1980.

7. McCain, Thomas A. and Victor D. Wall, Jr., "A Communication Perspective of a School Board Failure," *Educational Administration Quarterly*, XII, Spring 1976.
8. Newmark, Barbara D., "A School District Decides: A Successful Campaign Strategy," *Phi Delta Kappa*, November 1982.
9. Panas, Jerold, "But some districts still *do* win school referendums," *American School Board Journal*, March 1971.
10. Rochwell, Carolton C., "Secrets of Successful Seekers Call the Shots Yourself," *American Libraries*, November 1977.
11. Tonigan, Richard, "How to pass the bonds to get the plants to keep maintained," *School Management*, July 1971.

The variables listed in the following table were those shown in the literature (Bainbridge 1979, Keith and Braito 1974) to have a consistent relationship to the outcome of the bond/levy elections.

Table 2
Descriptive Variables Related to Bond/Levy Elections

Variable	Relationship
United school board	Positive
Positive community attitude toward Administration and Board	Positive
Having children in the school system	Positive
Older population	Negative
Having preschool age children	Negative
The higher income levels ($25,000+)	Positive
The lower income levels ($15,000−)	Negative
Education (high school diploma +)	Positive
Less than five years' education	Negative
Employed in education	Positive
Employed in government	Positive
Employed in professional roles	Positive
Employed in sales	Positive
Employed in construction	Negative
Employed in manufacturing	Negative
Employed as craftsman	Negative
Nonwhite population	Positive
Housewives	Positive
Organized opposition	Negative

Notes on Table 2

While the research on the size of the levy is inconclusive at this time, studies report both positive and negative relationships. The length of the levy is apparently positively related to success. That is, the longer the period of the levy, the more positive the voters are. Bainbridge attributes this to the possibility of a "success breeds success" syndrome. It appears that the more successful districts tend to request this type of levy.

The variables of amount of income and amount of education tend to follow the same pattern; as the amount increases, the voters become more positive.

It is probably no surprise that those who have children in the school system tend to be positive voters, but Bainbridge also found that parents of preschool age children tended to be negative, with the exception of those whose children were in nursery school. Apparently, having the children in some type of schooling has a positive influence on the voting attitude. Bainbridge suggests that young married couples with small children may be at the lower middle-income levels that have a negative influence on their vote. Also, these may be more mobile families who don't plan to be in the community long enough for their children to attend school. As a result, they have less commitment to the schools.

Renters are more positive voters than homeowners. Perhaps the renters do not see themselves as directly paying property taxes. Nonwhite voters tend to be more positive than white voters, perhaps because they see the schools as an opportunity for advancement. Interestingly, however, their voting participation is less.

In summary:

1. the longer the period of the levy, the more positive the voters are;
2. renters are more positive than homeowners; and,
3. while the nonwhite voters tend to be more positive than white voters, they participate less.

A Word of Caution

Tables 1 and 2 are intended as aids in hypothesis formulation. What is true for one community may not be for another. It is crucial to determine a community's own characteristics and to test and follow up on the campaign strategies employed.